This book is written for the education practitioner, who's actively engaged in teaching and learning within K–12 classrooms and wants to better understand their own experiences to help their students uncover meaning in theirs. This book is also for the school leader, who wants to set the example and uncover their own academic identity and navigate through the Entry Points of Equity with their staff and school community at large. I see the importance of this text for school leadership teams, to engage in the real conversations on how to move all teaching and learning practices toward more equitable systems for all students. In short, everyone in education needs to read this.

—Rebecca Davis-Dobson
Educator

The balance of qualitative storytelling combined with reflective practices is brilliant. This book covers vital topics, the practice of reflecting on equity, mindset, blind spots, microaggressions, and academic identities. The author draws you quickly into a space of vulnerability, and the structure of the book allows you to connect with the stories and reflect on your own academic identity, messages you may have received from your family, educators, peers, and how that has impacted your own journey with equity. The structure allows you to become curious about potential biases or microaggressions you may have about yourself or others.

—Piper Sherman Nichols
Clark County Region 2 Leadership Support, NWEA

The six entry points support moving all students forward that they may have a quality of life in the future that spells *success* and not *failure* based on the assumptions, attitudes, and biases of the general public or society. Equity has always been an issue, however, the light was shined on it again when the pandemic came up, as a way to say, we have *not* solved this issue; let's dig deeper. This publication can be another opportunity to dig deeper.

—Mitzi Mack
Librarian

# THE EQUITY EXPRESSION

*To my first and best teachers, my Dad and Mom.*

*To my ancestors, my words are the voice of your souls.*

*To our young people, may we always continue to learn from you!*

# THE EQUITY EXPRESSION

## Six Entry Points for Nonnegotiable Academic Success

FENESHA HUBBARD

A Joint Publication

CORWIN    nwea

FOR INFORMATION:

Corwin
A Sage Company
2455 Teller Road
Thousand Oaks, California 91320
(800) 233-9936
www.corwin.com

Sage Publications Ltd.
1 Oliver's Yard
55 City Road
London EC1Y 1SP
United Kingdom

Sage Publications India Pvt. Ltd.
Unit No 323-333, Third Floor, F-Block
International Trade Tower Nehru Place
New Delhi 110 019
India

Sage Publications Asia-Pacific Pte. Ltd.
18 Cross Street #10-10/11/12
China Square Central
Singapore 048423

Vice President and Editorial
    Director:  Monica Eckman
Program Director and Publisher:
    Dan Alpert
Acquisitions Editor:  Megan Bedell
Content Development Manager:
    Lucas Schleicher
Content Development Editor:
    Mia Rodriguez
Senior Editorial Assistant:
    Natalie Delpino
Editorial Intern:  Lex Nunez
Production Editor:  Melanie Birdsall
Copy Editor:  Jared Leighton
Typesetter:  Exeter Premedia Services
Proofreader:  Christine Dahlin
Cover Designer:  Janet Kiesel
Marketing Manager:  Melissa Duclos

ISBN 978-1-0718-9994-6

This book is printed on acid-free paper.

23 24 25 26 27 10 9 8 7 6 5 4 3 2 1

# CONTENTS

This is my first experience with an author who is thinking about equity through a lens to positively impact all students. It is a book for practitioners willing to tackle hard truths through reflective exercises that allow participants to reach into their deepest layers of self to identify what they believe, why they believe it, and what can be done, so they can work strategically toward a uniform solution. Readers will be captivated by the nonthreatening way in which the author challenges all of us to look at ourselves and to do better, while offering a set of tools to identify problems of practice as well as creating strong implementation plans through the six entry points for equity. Practitioners, leaders, and adults committed to helping students will be interested in this book, as it puts the onus of learning on educators while also providing concrete sequential steps needed to work toward meaningful solutions, and ultimately to embed equity into every learning culture.

—Tara Isaacs

... there's no single answer that will solve all of our future problems. There's no magic bullet. Instead there are thousands of answers—at least. You can be one of them if you choose to be.
—Octavia E. Butler, "A Few Rules for Predicting the Future,"
*Essence Magazine,* May 2000

# ACKNOWLEDGMENTS

This book started as a position statement for equity that evolved into a series of professional learning workshops for teachers. It takes courage to be a conduit for the people, especially when your ways of thinking differ from the norm. I am grateful for the educators across the nation that I've worked with the past two decades that welcomed me into their classrooms, schools, and hearts. They were always willing to join me in thinking about things differently and approaching learning from a new perspective. Their love of teaching and passion for learning are key factors in the equity expression.

The COVID-19 pandemic seemed to take months from my life, thus interrupting the writing of this book. I am fortunate to have family and friends that always support my ideas, stand by me, and cheer me on. Their support helped me bring *The Equity Expression* to life. I appreciate my sister and friend Aleata Hubbard Cheuoua—she is the smartest woman I know, and often she knows me better than I know myself. Aleata, thank you for always helping me to be my best self. I am extremely and forever grateful for my Dad and sisterfriends, especially Lynjunita Matsey, for keeping me nurtured, sane, and taken care of while writing this book. And for my coach, Dawn Albert, who helped me make sense of my writing journey and continued professional growth.

Thank you to my editors Dan Alpert and Megan Bedell for believing in my vision, and to Jacob Bruno for trusting my leadership. I am so grateful for the compassion and encouragement from Jaime Vazquez, who constantly reminded me that my voice needed to be heard. I work alongside wonderfully talented designers that make this content come alive, and I am so appreciative of you—Amber McKinney, Erin Beard, Joyce Smith, and Wendy St. Michell.

Very special thanks to my team at NWEA for giving me the space and tools to create with structure and soul. I am grateful to work with an organization that supports innovation in education. There are too many people at NWEA to name, but among those that helped ensure the success of this project are the following (those who are also contributors are noted with an asterisk):

| | | |
|---|---|---|
| Amber McKinney* | Joanne Luzietti | Simona Beattie |
| Amy Schmidt | Joyce Smith | Staci Kimmons |
| Chase Nordengren | Kim Baker | Tammy Baumann |
| Erin Beard* | Melissa Johnston | Vicki McCoy |
| Fred McDaniel | Monica Rodriguez | Vicki Rodriguez |
| Jacob Bruno | Rebecca Davis-Dobson | Wendy St. Michell* |
| Jaime Vazquez | Sharron Stroman | Yolanda Wallace |

Thank you to everyone who contributed their stories* to *The Equity Expression*.

| | | |
|---|---|---|
| Anita Brown | Mary Resanovich | Tami Hunter |
| Erin Washington | Moira Judd | Tara Isaacs |
| Greg King | Nick Joe | Vicky Tusken |
| Lisa Lee | Sarah Whitney | |

Alex Rozga, your design of the entry points for equity graphic is excellent. Thank you.

## PUBLISHER'S ACKNOWLEDGMENTS

Corwin gratefully acknowledges the contributions of the following reviewers:

Melissa A. Campbell
*K–5 Mathematics Specialist, Alabama Math, Science, and Technology Initiative*
*The University of Alabama in Huntsville*
*Huntsville, AL*

Rebecca Davis-Dobson
*Educator*
*Chicago, IL*

Mitzi Mack
*Librarian*
*Tampa, FL*

Saundra Mouton
*International Baccalaureate Coordinator, Reading Specialist*
*Briarmeadow Charter School*
*Katy, TX*

Piper Sherman Nichols
*Clark County Region 2 Leadership Support, NWEA*
*Las Vegas, NV*

Aspen Rendon
*Partner in Equity, Culture, and Community Engagement*
*Cherry Creek School District*
*Aurora, CO*

# INTRODUCTION

Everyone is talking about equity in education, and the topic is leading to ideological conflicts, changes in legislation, and culture wars. Teachers are charged with enacting equity, but they are overwhelmed by the immediate needs of the classroom. School leaders are still gaining clarity on the instructional connections to equity and district leaders are trying to communicate a vision and develop action around equity. Equity work is complex and sometimes hard. Simply talking about equity is difficult. *The Equity Expression* is a guide for equity conversations, and a tool to empower you as an equity change agent.

I will not assume that you and I have a shared understanding of equity, so let's begin by clarifying what we mean by equity throughout this book. **Equity** comprises the actions, beliefs, and behaviors that work together to identify and eliminate barriers to access and opportunities. In the case of K–12 education, equity is what gives the fair treatment, access, opportunity, and advancement to students and educators in a way that facilitates their individual success and belonging.

Most equity conversations can be circled back to the roots of systemic racism, a weed that has run rampant in our country. Some people choose to keep watering those weeds, others are pruning them to placate emotions around the topic, and many educators are working to eradicate the weeds altogether. Equity is a very personal topic and our instructional moves, whether equitable or inequitable, have great impact on students. Although the personal is political, please note that this book is not about the politicization of equity but rather about the deep inner work needed to have conversations around equity that will lead to equitable decision making for students.

*The Equity Expression* will help you think about equity from a different perspective, center equity in teaching and learning, and it will position you to engage in deep reflection and dialogue about equity. This book is written for classroom teachers but is also applicable to district leaders, administrators, support staff, and stakeholders whose decision making directly influences students.

**Mindsets**

**Systems**

**Relationships**

# 6 Entry Points for Equity

**Processes**

**Products**

**Spaces**

Source: NWEA, 2023. Used with permission.

Equity is a big topic. It can be challenging to address all the facets of equity—such as bias, access, -isms, inclusion—while meeting the needs of students, teachers, families, and communities. Although educators and stakeholders may share the intention of partnering to help all students learn, we each have different lenses, perspectives, and contexts through which we view situations and experiences. To meet this daunting challenge, we use the Entry Points for Equity.

Opportunities for equitable teaching and learning are everywhere. Entry points help you highlight where those opportunities are—and provide starting points where those opportunities don't exist. The six entry points I've identified help you access your understanding of, and experiences with equity—mindsets, relationships, products, spaces, processes, and systems. The entry points approach to equity focuses on helping educators identify starting points for equity conversations and key things to consider for decision making.

## WHAT THIS BOOK IS AND WHAT IT ISN'T

This book isn't a blueprint for how to solve your school, district, and community equity issues. This book isn't about how to fix all of the problems stemming from hundreds of years of an oppressive business model of slavery in our country. *The Equity Expression* will help you talk about equity differently, as it will challenge you to reimagine discourse on equity at the confluence of high-quality instructional content and an excellent and equitable education.

*The Equity Expression* will help you examine how equity, or the lack thereof, manifests in K–12 education, but it's going to take a different approach to the equity conversation. This book is about how you can enact change by starting from within. Our brains are wired for stories and equity work requires that we be more qualitative in our approach to research, which is why this book will take a conversational tone. Research is respected and referenced throughout this book, but the most important research is happening now in our nation's classrooms every single day.

In this book, I share first-person examples from my twenty-year career as an educator, as well as examples from the lived experiences of other teachers. I shared these experiences to provide insight that can help us all grow in ways that help us better serve our students, not to condemn. Vulnerability through storytelling is hard, and it doesn't always feel comfortable. But stories of self-disclosure are what help us connect to the humanity in one another. If we see ourselves as equity change agents, then we need to start by owning the contexts and identities that we bring to our work.

In other words, if we get vulnerable, and self-reflective, we can start to find opportunities to make our efforts and experiences more equitable. I want you to use the stories in this book to strengthen empathy for our students and fellow educators. I hope that this book will help you gain more compassion for yourself as an equity empowered educator. I know that the exercises and tools that accompany the entry points will encourage you to put equity into action.

## HOW DO I USE THE ENTRY POINTS FOR EQUITY?

This book will help you understand how to navigate the entry points so that you can best guide students on their journey of learning. Imagine that you and your colleagues are traveling along parallel roads. Each road has roundabouts that give you opportunities to redirect your path. The roundabouts appear as you continuously grow and improve in your practice. Each road and path inevitably leads to student success. The instructional decisions we make pave the roads, and the paths present themselves as entry points—opportunities to enact equity in a way that better informs your instructional decisions. Regardless of the path taken, you are always headed toward student success. Wouldn't you want to travel this road?

Whether your answer is yes, no, or maybe, keep reading because this book provides you with an opportunity to expand your thinking around equity. Someone else reading this text is likely thinking that this is just another book on equity, and that they've heard it all before. Let me assure you that using the entry points to make equity actionable in your work is not about doing anything new. Rather, it's about thinking differently, entering the equity conversation from another perspective, and closing the gap between having knowledge about equity and putting it into action with intention and focus. The entry points for equity can support you and your learning team in taking ownership of equity and will help you know when and why to exit the roundabout.

## START WITH MINDSETS AND ACADEMIC IDENTITIES

The entry points for equity are designed to be employed when deemed timely, relevant, and meaningful for students. If we truly believe in partnering to help our students learn, then their most immediate needs will dictate where we need to grow and in which direction we should go (i.e., which entry point). You do not have to address the entry points in any specific order, although it's important to note that the entry points are anchored around mindsets, which is the foundation for all other entry points.

Educators' mindsets are directly correlated to their academic identity, assumptions, and biases, and this connection is further explained through the stories and examples in this book. You are probably familiar with identity as it relates to culture, gender, or socioeconomic status, to name a few types of identities that play a part in the multiple systems of oppression at work in K–12 education—from culture wars to the **school-to-prison pipeline**. At the time of writing this book, I identify as a Black woman, so I have a strong affinity to things such as my hair and language that affirm this cultural identity (although this affinity is not unique to being a Black woman). Rooted in my cultural identity is my personal belief that I have the responsibility to empower young girls to feel confident in how they choose to express themselves through hair styles and language choices. This belief has led me to take actions such as mentoring and teaching young girls.

I once had an **academic identity** that was full of unhealthy ideas about math. As a young math student, I found that I could follow the processes and formulas of math, but I wasn't great with the mechanics when it came to problem-solving. If you asked me to explain how to solve a particular math problem, I could describe the right ideas, and why they were important. My ways of thinking about and doing math were usually not affirmed and guided, nor considered within success criteria, which indirectly told me that

I was not a good or successful math student. When it came to following a specific method for solving problems, I would fumble, and ultimately, the parts that I did get about math got lost. I developed an academic identity that associated math success with rote operations. I learned, indirectly, that the rules of math were more important than inquiry and exploration. Those ideas were not healthy because I experienced math as a rigid, linear process, and as a creative person, that made math less accessible to me.

> *Academic identities are not fixed. It is imperative that we (educators) continue to expand our academic identities through professional learning and reflection.*

Academic identities are not fixed. It is imperative that we (educators) continue to expand our academic identities through professional learning and reflection. In the first two chapters of this book, you will uncover your academic identity as a learner, explore how it has impacted your teaching, and learn to navigate the entry points for equity guide. Much of the initial work will allow you to dive deeply and more easily into the other entry points for equity.

The reason I make a connection between the entry point of mindsets and a person's academic identity is because decisions and actions are a result of a belief or behavior. Empowering beliefs about teaching and learning can lead to actions that can have a positive impact on our students. This directly relates to equity in K–12 because all educational decisions impact the teaching and learning experiences of students. I believe that decisions rooted in right thinking will lead to right actions. This book will help ensure that your actions are equitable for all. If you choose to implement the strategies in *The Equity Expression*, you'll be on your way to championing equity for all.

Understanding your own beliefs about teaching, learning, content, pedagogy, and students is essential to operationalizing equity. What is your identity as an educator? Your academic identity, or the dispositions and beliefs that make up your relationship with education, shapes your teaching and learning experiences. I was lucky that I became aware of my math academic identity early on and was able to reflect on how it could influence my instruction. Once I became a math teacher, I was able to employ strategies to help all students thrive in the mathematics classroom.

Our academic identities are constantly being shaped and developed. Our understanding and enactment of equity expands as we grow and change. By applying the entry points to your work, I believe you will begin to transform your practice in ways that result in increased self-determination and intrinsic motivation among young people, which will lead to greater student outcomes.

# GETTING THE MOST OUT OF THIS BOOK

Examining equity in K–12 education is important for people who want to create more fair and unbiased learning experiences for students. The chapters in this book progress from self-examination to bigger topics, allowing you to see how we can close the equity knowing–doing gap at the classroom level and how system-level changes can be accessible to teachers and administrators. The purpose of this book is to provide you with a framework through which you can operationalize equity. I want this book to serve as a compass that allows you to personalize your equity work, with greater agency. My intention is to prepare you to engage in deep reflection and dialogue about equity. As such, there are activities, tools, and reflections in each chapter. Also, I've invited a few of my educator friends to join you on this journey. They will provide thoughts and insights throughout the book, to support your inner dialogue and prepare you for conversations with other educators.

# HOW TO USE THIS BOOK

## Teachers

I wrote this book for educators that lead classrooms and work directly with students. It's also for educators who have lost (or never had) a belief in equity; those who have been unjustly treated by having the very things that can empower our students (i.e., data) used against them (i.e., for evaluation); or for those who may have deficit-focused or disempowering beliefs that they've never fully examined (i.e., that "those" children aren't capable). The best way for teachers to use this book is to

1. Complete the activities and answer the questions
2. Focus on one entry point at a time and
3. Dive deeper into the content with a community, such as your grade band colleagues or peers

## Instructional Coaches and Leaders

Instructional coaches and leaders will also benefit from doing the work in this book, as it will help them lead discussions around equity in schools. I consulted with a seasoned educator and asked her to provide me with suggestions on how to best support others as they use this book to guide their equity journey. Below are her tips for you:

- If you're doing this work as professional development or in a professional learning community, the facilitator needs to read the whole book in advance and think about potential types of reactions they may encounter. For each chapter they might identify common questions or areas where participants might push back and think about how they might respond to help shift participant thinking.

- Teachers are really stressed right now, so having an easy way for them to engage with the book is important. Some ways to do this are

  o **Ask teachers what they need.** The book is conducive to writing, yet some teachers might find a video or audio recording a more appealing way to record their thoughts. *How can I support you as a facilitator? How can we support each other as a group? How might teachers like to record or share their reflection?*

  o **Assess teachers' needs prior to reading.**

    ▪ What scares you about this work?

    ▪ What excites you about this work?

    ▪ Describe your experience with equity-focused professional learning.

    ▪ What can we do to make this a safe space for self-exploration?

  o **Hold regular meetings to discuss each chapter.** At the end of each meeting, I think it would be useful to preview the chapter to come (maybe tease something to hook participants, even read an excerpt), and specify the number of reflections and estimated amount of time to complete reflections.

  o **Brainstorm with teachers what will help them stay up to date with readings.** Consider assigning accountability buddies, issuing weekly reminders, and creating an online chat board to share takeaways and ideas.

  o **Fortune is in the follow-up.** After reading each chapter, encourage participants to look for examples of the entry point discussed within their classroom. Teachers should be prepared to share what they notice and wonder the next time you meet as a group. As a culminating project, the group could choose to focus on one entry point to try to implement a change.

## FOCUS OF EACH CHAPTER

Here is what is covered in each chapter:

**Chapter 1: Academic Identities**—Through a series of reflective activities, you will explore how your experiences as a learner and educator have shaped how you think about, engage with, and what you believe about education.

**Chapter 2: Mindsets**—As you and your learning team use the Entry Points for Equity, I encourage you to begin always with mindsets. This chapter will help you explore how mindsets impact academic identities.

**Chapters 3 and 4: Relationships**—These chapters will center the importance of building and maintaining psychologically safe relationships with other educators and students so that you can amplify your agency as an equity-empowered educator.

**Chapter 5: Products**—You'll learn equity look-fors in the tools used to support teaching and learning, and understand the role of cultural responsiveness in products to reflect the ideas and experiences learners will recognize.

**Chapter 6: Processes**—In this chapter, you'll learn how you can enact equity through teaching and learning processes, while letting day-to-day classroom practices guide your steps.

**Chapter 7: Spaces**—This chapter will help you examine the environments created for learning and the messages these spaces convey to learners.

**Chapter 8: Systems**—Be inspired by fellow educators with advice on how to thrive in systems fraught with inequities.

**Chapter 9: Activating the Entry Points**—Learn how to begin to put equity into action with a structured framework and examples. This chapter will give you opportunities to process and make sense of the entry points.

## WHAT DO I NEED TO KNOW AS I READ THIS BOOK?

The three concepts that I want you to know and further understand as you read this book are these:

1. **Equity—*What it is:*** Equity is the fair treatment, access, opportunity, and advancement for students and educators that facilitate their individual success and belonging. ***What it does:*** Equity identifies and eliminates the barriers to access and opportunities that put students at a disadvantage.

2. **Academic Identity**—The dispositions and beliefs that make up a person's relationship with teaching, learning, and educational topics or subjects.

3. **Entry Points for Equity Guide**—A tool designed to help guide discussions and decision making around equity as it relates to mindsets, relationships, products, spaces, processes, and systems in K–12 education.

Your understanding of these key terms will continue to evolve as you do equity work. Allow yourself grace as you learn and grow. I provide a reflective opportunity in each chapter for you to circle back to these key concepts and reflect on your new learning. Let's practice with a reflection:

# REFLECTION

Use the space below to reflect on the key concepts of equity, academic identity, and entry points for equity framework.

- How do the definitions of these concepts connect to what you already know?
- How do the definitions fit with or disrupt your current thinking?
- What are the natural relationships between equity and academic identities?

_____

_____

_____

_____

_____

The entry points for equity are designed to make equity accessible and actionable. As you grow in your equity work, so will your understanding of equity. Some topics may be new to you, and some you will find easy to apply in other ways. I encourage you to start where you are, with what you have, and hold an intention to create better outcomes for students whenever and wherever you enter the equity conversation.

## GROWTH AND DEVELOPMENT TOOLS

> "Begin to see with the eye behind the eye. Hear with the ear behind the ear. Feel with the heart behind the heart. So [you] can see the invisible, hear the inaudible, do the impossible."
>
> —Michael Bernard Beckwith

It is imperative that you allow time to process and make sense of ideas presented in this book. Reflection exercises are built into each chapter, which will help you connect with your inner self, and your team, as you engage in equity work. The reflections that you share in this guide are true for YOU, so it is important that you honor your truths by writing them down and going deeper to make sense of why they are your truths. You must respond with honesty and vulnerability in order for the exercises in this book to work. I trust you to do that. (And I also understand that sometimes it's hard to find the words right away. In that case, let your hand doodle on the page as the ideas move from your heart to your head, and onto the paper.)

The exercises and activities will help you examine the messy stuff that comes up as you reflect on your equity work, ideate possibilities for growth and change, and co-create solutions with your colleagues that will lead to improved student outcomes. *The Equity Expression* will help you feel more prepared to have difficult and necessary conversations with your team.

Yes, you'll feel hopeful and optimistic while doing your equity work, but it will not be easy. Equity work is hard. Face it—you're going to uncover some assumptions, biases, and beliefs that you didn't know you held. Face it—you're going to learn things about your colleagues that you wish you could unlearn. Face it—you're going to get vulnerable, which might make you feel raw and exposed. Face it—you are going to use all of this information to grow forward and the outcome will not only be a better you, but better teaching and learning for our students. Utilizing the four steps below will challenge you to FACE it:

1.  Facts and Feelings: Identify the facts and name the feelings that arise in you from those facts.

2.  Agree and Argue: State what you agree with and what you would argue.

3.  Connections: Draw parallels to your own experiences.

4.  Epiphanies: Record your "aha's" and takeaways.

**If you are using this book in professional development:** Please complete the activities in each chapter prior to meeting with your team, PLC, or before attending the equity workshops that align with the book.

## AGREEMENTS

In order for this book to work for you, I ask that you commit to the following:

*As an equity-focused educator committed to personal growth and professional development in order to better serve our students—*

- *I will make time to complete the exercises in this book.*
- *I will tell the truth, with compassion for myself and others.*
- *I will not pass judgment on others, nor on myself.*
- *I will be willing to hear, and try to understand, other people's perspectives.*
- *I will be open to changing limiting beliefs into empowering beliefs.*

Consider committing to these rules of engagement as you have courageous conversations with your colleagues:

- *I will assume good intent.*
- *I will listen without preparing to respond.*
- *I will seek to understand, then to be understood.*
- *I accept that there may be more questions than answers.*
- *I expect that closure may not be reached.*

## YOUR EXPECTATIONS

Being clear on your expectations will help set you up for a successful journey as you read this book. Based on the introduction, how might you grow as a result of engaging with *The Equity Expression*? After writing your answer, read the responses from your fellow educators to see what aligns with your expectations. If you find that someone's response differs from yours, consider rereading portions of the introduction and then revisit your answer.

## REFLECTION

What type of learning do you expect to experience as you read *The Equity Expression?*

_____

_____

_____

_____

_____

 **Teacher Commentary**

▶ Based on what I've just read, I will be using the anchor of mindsets to look at our identity as educators and how that affects our instruction and the way we treat and teach our students. I will need to be honest with myself if I want to get the full value of the learning presented in this book.

(Continued)

*(Continued)*

There will be exercises that I will need to do and I will need to make sure to not judge those teachers who are not on the same page as myself.

▶ This introduction makes it very clear that engaging with this book first and foremost involves a personal reflective journey, that will require honesty and vulnerability on the part of the participant (notice I am not referring to the person reading the book "the reader"). The introduction also makes it very clear that this is not a book providing tools and tips on how to create the "perfect equitable" classroom.

▶ Based on the intro, this book is about making equity actionable through the six entry points, examining oneself with lots of self-reflection, and tapping into my academic identities and mindsets as an educator.

▶ I expect to reflect on my personal experiences, clearly defining equity, assigning meaning to equity (locating where I am and would like to be), examining my actions while utilizing an equity framework to inform planning practice and high-quality instruction for all students.

▶ I expect to examine my actions while utilizing an equity framework to inform planning practice and high-quality instruction for all students.

▶ This book makes me think a lot about the airplane safety talk I receive before flying. "In the event of an emergency oxygen masks will drop from the ceiling. . . . Put on your mask before helping others." Another way to think about that is that any exercise in helping inform practice needs to start with informing oneself. I have a feeling that this is going to involve a lot of learning and unlearning my blind spots in order to truly lean into enhancing equity with others.

 **Teacher Pro-Tip**

I love these activities and I feel like they can be emotionally taxing and take up a lot of cognitive space. You should give yourself space and time in between some of these activities so that the quality of your responses doesn't diminish. I suggest you take time to stop and take a breath, go on a nature walk, listen to some music, and then return to the book. Chapter 1 really helps you dig into academic identities and gets to the heart of where your mindsets lie. It requires intense self-reflection. You will want to spend time on this chapter and take it in chunks. This is arguably the most important (and hardest) part of the book, but it's worth it! It will require you to dig up memories you thought you forgot, perspectives you never had before, and traumas you buried deep down inside.

Equity will always be a key component of teaching and learning. May the examples, strategies, tools, and resources in this book help guide you along your equity journey with ease, clarity, and optimism.

# CHAPTER 1

........................................

# ACADEMIC IDENTITIES

> *"It is important for teachers to understand the impact of the instructional decisions that they make, and the social and academic norms that they create, on a child's [academic] identity."*
>
> —*Julia Aguirre, Karen Mayfield-Ingram, and Danny Bernard Martin*, The Impact of Identity in K–8 Mathematics

One of the greatest inequities I experienced as a learner was teaching that used an instructional model that supported a checklist mindset, thinking of math as facts and procedures to be memorized. I often wonder, How would an equity lens among my teachers have shaped my learning experience differently? Rather than teaching one way of solving a problem, what would my learning have been like if my teachers encouraged me to find different solution methods? I wonder what type of student I would have been in a math classroom where curiosity and questioning were encouraged, where getting the wrong answer was expected along the learning journey (and not always penalized), and various ways of thinking were celebrated. In this environment, the teacher would have had a mindset that all students are capable of learning, and I, as a student, would have had faith in my own intellectual capacity. I would have a healthy, empowering academic identity. This is growth mindset at its best.

Understanding how our academic identities impact teaching and learning is one way to begin to address equity. Cultivating a healthy academic identity and mindset is an ongoing process. If you reach the point where you feel that you can't grow any further, then you've restricted the intellectual spaces to which you and your students can go. In this chapter, we will begin to unpack your academic identity, which will reveal some of the factors that contribute to what you choose to teach, how you teach it, and what you believe about the students that you teach. This chapter will help strengthen your self-reflective techniques and unearth your academic identity by focusing on four key questions:

1. Why do you teach?
2. Why do you teach what you teach?
3. What is your academic identity?
4. What is your dominant academic identity?

**academic identity:** The dispositions and beliefs that make up a person's relationship with teaching, learning, and educational topics or subjects

## WHY DO YOU TEACH?

Why do you teach? You want to impact lives. You love teaching others how to learn. You want to change the educational system for the better. You live for the lightbulb moments in the classroom. The joy and innocence of youth inspires you to teach. You teach to make a difference. Most educators can tell you why they engage in the profession of teaching, and the reason is usually connected to a purpose bigger than themselves. Our *why* for teaching usually details the impact and influence we can have on students. Our purpose for teaching is often to cultivate young minds.

The key to sustainability in this profession is to be driven by your *why*. It is acceptable for your *why* to include extrinsic factors such as the benefits of teaching that enhance your professional growth, the financial support that teaching provides for you and your family, or the systemic ways that teaching allows you to make a difference, such as volunteering or leading community events. Equally important are the intrinsic factors that add value to your *why*, such as the beliefs you hold about teaching and your expectations of what teaching should entail. These intrinsic factors are directly connected to your mindset, which is our first entry point for equity.

Here is a story about a teacher whose *why* was strengthened by her students:

*I had an overwhelmingly positive academic identity as a student, but unfortunately that had a negative impact during my first few years of teaching. I entered the profession with the assumption that because I had such a healthy academic identity I was best positioned to develop that in my students. I thought it would be easy because my intentions were good and I was in it for the right reasons. I quickly saw that I had to empathize with students who had negative academic identities and work to help them see the possibility of a more positive identity. It was a team effort, though, because the impact of another teacher's mindsets and/or actions could carry over into my classroom and vice versa. This is another reason this work is important: one teacher may be able to make ripples, but it takes a team to change the tide.*

Teaching is a profession that could benefit from a shared value proposition, or an agreed-upon promise of what will we do for and with students. Doctors take the Hippocratic Oath, swearing to uphold medical standards for patients. Police officers' oath of honor details how to serve and protect communities. Teachers? Well, we're getting there—from making sure no child is left behind (NCLB, 2002) to ensuring that every student succeeds (ESSA, 2015), students seem to be the *why* that drives education reform. However, we don't take an oath when we start teaching, and there is no shared agreement that drives our work.

Perhaps one of the reasons we don't have a shared value proposition in education is because we misconstrue the essential terms that define our work. According to Sir Ken Robinson, Ph.D., and Kate Robinson, we often conflate and confuse the terms learning, education, training, and school. "Learning is the process of acquiring new skills and understanding. Education is an organized system of learning. Training is a type of education that is focused on learning specific skills. A school is a community of learners: a group that comes together to learn with and from each other. It is vital that we differentiate these terms: children love to learn, they do it naturally; many have a hard time with education, and some have big problems with school" (Robinson & Robinson, 2022).

Does this distinction change your response to the question *why do you teach?* If so, record your enhanced response below:

**Why do you teach?**

Insert your answer here: _____

**Teacher Commentary**

▶ It's easy for me to give the typical answer—"I want to make a difference." But, in all honesty, I got into teaching originally to support my family and specifically pay for my children's education. After a few years, I discovered that I had an inner calling to pursue this vocation. I never call teaching my profession or career.

(Continued)

*(Continued)*

▶ When thinking of teachers' academic identities and often how I perceived their identities, especially in times of frustration around damaging words or actions that lacked sensitivity and/or promoted inequities, I often had to remind myself that all teachers got into teaching because they care about kids. We know teachers aren't in it for the money or the great hours. They truly got into it because of their love of kids. With that in mind, I also had to remember that teachers' academic identities were fluid and that I could have a positive effect on kids by helping change their biases.

## WHY DO YOU TEACH WHAT YOU TEACH?

You've identified why you teach, and now I want you to consider why you teach the subject(s) that you teach. Understanding how our subjects connect to the various dimensions of learning gives us greater purpose in our teaching. In *The Impact of Identity in K–8 Mathematics*, former middle and high school teacher Julia Marie Aguirre et al. "[encourages] all teachers to reflect on three questions: What mathematics? For whom? For what purposes?" The authors "contend that deep meaningful reflection on these questions will require teachers to examine their beliefs about learners, learning and mathematics content as well as their everyday teaching and classroom practices" (Aguirre et al., 2013). Let's consider other subjects. For example, why do you teach science? For what purpose are students learning history? What do students gain by learning art? Why do you teach math? Who is math for?

As you think about those questions, keep in mind that the purpose of schooling has changed with society. What was once an institution for instilling American values then transformed to one designed to keep our nation on the cutting edge of math, science, and technology. The changes in society have illuminated the need for schools to be an avenue through which we give all students equal opportunity to thrive as citizens. While the role of school is constantly changing, keeping students at the center of teaching, learning, and schooling appears to remain constant.

Let's examine your beliefs about teaching through the lens of what academic and author Geneva Gay calls **culturally responsive teachers**. More specifically, Dr. Gay says, "Culturally responsive teachers have unequivocal faith in the human dignity and intellectual capabilities of their students. They view learning as having intellectual, academic, personal, social, ethical, and political dimensions, all of which are developed in concert with one another." Take about 15 to 30 minutes to complete the following table, capturing your initial reactions in rapid-fire form and then revisiting each section with deeper consideration.

## Why Do We Teach Specific Subjects?

Identify one or two reasons that explain how, in your opinion, each dimension connects to the subject listed. For example, you might say that the social dimension connects to history because it helps students understand other cultures and develop cultural tolerance.

|  | SCIENCE | MATH | READING | ELA | HISTORY | MUSIC | (INSERT YOUR SUBJECT HERE) |
|---|---|---|---|---|---|---|---|
| Academic |  |  |  |  |  |  |  |
| Personal |  |  |  |  |  |  |  |
| Social |  |  |  |  |  |  |  |
| Ethical |  |  |  |  |  |  |  |
| Political |  |  |  |  |  |  |  |

## WHAT'S YOUR ACADEMIC IDENTITY?

What does it mean to learn? To be a student? How does one acquire knowledge? The answers to all these questions compose the ideas and beliefs you hold about teaching and learning, which become evident in how you teach, what you teach, and the expectations you hold for students, all of which impact the way students perceive themselves as learners. The ideas and beliefs you hold about teaching and learning were likely formed when you were a young student. The way teachers and adults responded to your schoolwork, reactions you got from peers about the way you think, and grades you received are all examples of things that impacted your disposition toward school and specific subjects, your academic identity. When we help students become more aware of their academic identities, we can better affirm their ways of thinking about academic content and their ways of demonstrating what they know and don't know.

Now, let's begin to unpack your academic identity with a biography exercise. Set aside up to 20 minutes per sitting to respond to the following questions. Allow yourself time and space to process the answers that come up for you and revisit the questions later if needed. The purpose of this reflection activity is to capture your experiences, ideas, and beliefs about learning. Answer the questions that you feel most passionate about. You'll also practice exercising empathy for your students' experiences. Completing your educator biography is an empowering exercise. It can validate your experience and affirm your learning needs.

## Your Educator Biography

*As a K–12 student . . .*

1. How did you feel about school? Did you like or dislike it? Why did you feel that way?

2. What did it mean to be a successful student when you were in elementary school? Middle school? High school?

3. What types of grades did you get in school? Why?

4. What do you remember teachers or other adults saying about your capabilities as a student?

5. Who were the successful students in your classes? How did you know they were successful?

6. Describe your most memorable positive experiences in learning, inside or outside the classroom.

7. Describe your most memorable negative experiences in learning, inside or outside the classroom.

8. What factors are essential in helping students learn about and connect with academic content?

9. How have you seen students learn best?

After responding to the questions, imagine your younger self being asked, Who are you as a learner? If you probed your younger self to explore their academic identity and define the type of learner they are, what *I am* statements would your younger self make? Jot down the first ten *I am* statements that come to mind for you.

*As a K–12 student, my younger self would say . . .*

1. I am _____.
2. I am _____.
3. I am _____.
4. I am _____.
5. I am _____.
6. I am _____.
7. I am _____.
8. I am _____.
9. I am _____.
10. I am _____.

# REFLECTION

In what ways has the academic identity you had when you were a student impacted who you are as a teacher?

_____

_____

_____

_____

_____

_____

_____

_____

 **Teacher Commentary**

This activity was very eye opening! From kindergarten through eighth grade, my family moved every two years, so I was always new in school. My teachers said that I was so quiet, and they wished that I would talk more. School made me feel judged and monitored. I was not super-fond of other kids and found them mean and unreasonable. The kids who were successful were boys who learned quickly. I didn't like school and thought that it was boring, frustratingly repetitive, and somewhat nonsensical. I hated math but loved reading; it was an escape for me. It wasn't until I got to high school that I actually sort-of liked school. I went to a small, private high school that was very rooted in the arts. Because of the small size of the school and the classes, we had a much better sense of community. Each year, our history, literature, and art history classes focused on the same eras and cultures. We had discussions, did class projects, and wrote constantly. I spent two to four hours every night doing homework, but I never had to work that hard academically again in my life. Our teachers liked us, were experts in their subject matter, and were excited to teach us about it.

I grew up in foster care. People told me I was Jewish, but I lived in a Christian home. My personal and academic identities were always in conflict. I don't think any teachers knew what to do with me. I could read and memorize a book, but then I would fail all the exams. I didn't want anyone to know I was smart, yet I always wanted to prove that I could be smart. My behavior in school was often antithetical to my performance. My academic identity is a walking contradiction. I don't think I've grown out of that. I've started at the very bottom of any role in my career. I seem to lack all pedigree for success. I belong and also know I never will. There are moments where I'm thankful for the teachers I had, but also incredibly frustrated with the system that allowed me to move forward without being properly challenged or tended to. It's helpful to know that the systems we are working to redesign and retrain are ones that allow academic identities to be shifted in powerful and meaningful ways.

Reflecting on your experience as a student can be an affirming exercise if you access good memories and experiences. It can also bring up feelings of inadequacy or trigger memories that you tucked away because they were too painful to retain. Most importantly, your heightened awareness of the experiences that shaped you as a learner, coupled with insight on how those experiences impacted your teaching, helps you build empathy and greater understanding for your own students' learning experiences.

> *Your heightened awareness of the experiences that shaped you as a learner, coupled with insight on how those experiences impacted your teaching, helps you build empathy and greater understanding for your own students' learning experiences.*

## UNDERSTANDING OTHERS' ACADEMIC IDENTITIES

A teacher's academic identity is akin to their **pedagogical beliefs**, which can influence how and what they teach, their beliefs about students, and what they deem appropriate and necessary in relating to and working with colleagues and administrators. Understanding different academic identities is how we begin to address equity.

> *The perspective that teachers embrace has an impact on their view of their role and their effectiveness as educators (teacher identity) and subsequently governs the content that they teach and the instructional practices that they employ. Simply put, what teachers believe is important influences the decisions that they make about what content to teach, how to teach it, and in many cases, who*

*should receive the content. In this way, teaching is no different from many other areas in life. We make decisions on the basis of what we believe. (Aguirre et al., 2013, p. 58)*

Let's explore the academic identities of four teachers based on things they believed when they were a young learner and what they believe now as educators. View the profiles from the mindset that there is no good or bad teacher profile, no right or wrong way of thinking. A person's academic identity is not fixed; it changes over time as new thoughts and ideas come into the person's knowing.

> *A person's academic identity is not fixed; it changes over time as new thoughts and ideas come into the person's knowing. If you reach the point where you feel that you cannot grow any further, then you have restricted the intellectual spaces to which you and your students can go.*

## Teacher Profiles

| ELISE PATTON | |
|---|---|
| As a student, in the past: | If I liked a subject, then I enjoyed learning about it. My teachers made math fun. |
| As a teacher, today: | I think all students should experience a mix of conceptual understanding and procedural skill in mathematics. |

| PAMIR GALAGATE | |
|---|---|
| As a student, in the past: | I had a teacher call me stupid because of a mistake I made in class. I always tried to get the right answers. |
| As a teacher, today: | Students need to know and stick to the facts. Conceptual understanding and knowing why or how to apply the concepts is a waste of time. |

| DARNELL BOYD | |
|---|---|
| As a student, in the past: | Doing things on my own would cause me to get stuck in my head. I learned best when I was part of a group. |
| As a teacher, today: | Acceleration should come within the current grade level, and teachers should differentiate and scaffold in order to meet students at their level of readiness. |

| AISHA NELSON | |
|---|---|
| As a student, in the past: | I was a good student, and I liked learning new things. I could do work without having to ask an adult for help. |
| As a teacher, today: | Students should be allowed to skip a grade if it meets their learning and development needs. |

# REFLECTION

Select one of the teacher profiles and answer the following questions. Repeat the process for a different teacher profile.

1. How might this person have behaved in the classroom as a student? What might you see them do or say as a young student in the classroom?

   _____

   _____

   _____

2. What connections can you make between their beliefs as a student and their beliefs as a teacher?

   _____

   _____

   _____

3. What impact might their learning experience as a student have on their teaching style or instructional model?

   _____

   _____

   _____

4. Describe what you think each teacher's classroom looks like and sounds like on a typical day.

_____

_____

_____

Let's look at how some fellow educators feel about how their academic identities have changed during their teaching career and about growth as professional educators overall.

## Teacher Commentary

▶ My academic identity as a teacher has shifted greatly from when I started teaching over 10 years ago. When I first started, I definitely had a foundational academic identity in basically everything. I was super-focused on compliant students, a strong "I do, we do, you do" lesson structure, and mastery as shown by test scores. As I've moved to a firm academic identity, especially in elementary education, I now am focused on teaching the whole learner, especially their social-emotional learning; creating engaging lessons; empowering the student to lead their learning; and really focusing on the learning (rather than the teaching).

▶ When I first began teaching, I was more of a *learner manager* because that was the model I was most familiar with. Over time, with a lot of help from mentors, I shifted into becoming a *learner empowerer*.

▶ I see that I really tried to work the "secret rules of school" by being a well-behaved student with good relationships with teachers that focused on participation, group work, and homework for my grades that would make up for my poor mastery as shown in my test scores. As a teacher now, I know that students connect to relevant, engaging, and experiential content that gives process and problem-solving time. I realize that the factors that I now see as essential in helping students learn about and connect with academic content were not accessible to me in my classes. The academic environments that I was a part of were very lecture-based and focused on rote memorization.

▶ I become very sad when I see how "fixed" some teachers' identities are because my academic identity certainly has not been fixed! I've been in education for 31 years and all

(Continued)

*(Continued)*

of the roles I've held have immersed me into very different student demands and teaching practices. I've been a preschool teacher and elementary reading teacher in a southern state as well as a Title 1 and middle school language arts teacher in a fairly affluent district near a major city. I then went on to become a district-level curriculum coordinator. Each experience demanded from me very different things, and I chose to grow from every experience, rather than let it get me down or stuck.

▶ It is interesting that many of my teacher training experiences geared me up to be the "factory-model, compliance-oriented" teacher, even when they claimed to be doing the opposite. Or they'd still have policies and procedures that promote factory, compliance-based thinking. If this is the norm, then teachers doing equity work will be going against the grain. If this is the case, it's important to keep going because the end goal is to deliver an equitable education for students.

▶ Students assume that teachers enter the field because they were once good students (and, yes, many do for that reason). But not me! I once shared with my students how I struggled as a student and was often distracted, unmotivated, and underperforming. And as a result, I was the perfect candidate to be a middle school teacher. I brought a level of empathy for the student experience that many of my colleagues did not.

## THE TEACHER BECOMES THE STUDENT

Equitable instruction can create **student agency** and student motivation to facilitate success. Student agency is ownership of the learning. It's what gives students voice in how they learn, which empowers them to influence their own path to mastery. I encourage you to continue reflecting on your current practice and to assess how you might strengthen your academic identity to better influence student learning, which is one way we can place equity in the context of teaching and learning.

Here is an account from a high school math teacher that models the expansive opportunity for growth that can result from self-reflection. I sat down with Win Rodriguez, a high school math teacher, and asked her, "What experience as an educator impacted how you think about teaching and learning math? Why?" Below is Win's response.

> My name is Win Rodriguez, and I'm a high school math teacher. I loved math classes as a high school student, but I didn't feel affirmed as a student of math. Very few people in my classes (teachers and students) looked like me, and I struggled to solve problems following the methods taught in class. I didn't feel smart. Although I wanted to pursue a career as a math educator, my lack

24    THE EQUITY EXPRESSION

*of confidence led me to study marketing instead, then accounting. After a while, I became more confident in my abilities, and I obtained higher degrees in math along with a teaching certification. Twenty years of teaching high school math assured me that I had sound pedagogical content knowledge. I embodied the stereotype that high school math teachers had a deeper understanding of math. I prided myself on my ability to help students make sense of their mathematical thinking. One day, while working with a group of math coaches on the topic of fractions, a colleague asked me to help her with the division of fractions. I completed a problem using the standard algorithm: inverting the second fraction and multiplying both terms. My colleague affirmed that my answer and solution method were both correct, but she asked me why "invert and multiply" actually works. I was stumped and couldn't provide an answer! That was a pivotal point in my career as an educator because my level of conceptual understanding had been challenged. Up until that point, I had never questioned why things worked.*

Win didn't have a very healthy academic identity as a student because she struggled to perform in class and didn't feel smart. She was discouraged that none of her peers or teachers looked like her. Over time Win became self-empowered as she learned about marketing and accounting and experienced success in those fields. Win was feeling better about her intellectual capabilities and went on to be a successful math teacher of 20 years.

Then, Win experienced a third major shift in her academic identity. The shift occurred when she was challenged to have a greater conceptual understanding of her content area. Win had acquired a deep understanding of her subject matter, and when asked to explore her conceptual understanding, she discovered a gap in her knowledge. Without an in-depth understanding of why the algorithm worked, Win might have missed opportunities to help students make connections to bigger ideas and concepts. While she had strong subject matter expertise, Win's lack of in-depth conceptual understanding could prevent her from correcting students' possible misconceptions or from affirming her students' different ways of thinking about the math.

Although she had developed a healthy academic identity, an opportunity presented itself for Win to strengthen her pedagogical content knowledge — to "transform the content knowledge he or she possesses into forms that are pedagogically powerful and yet adaptive to the variations in ability and background presented by the students" (Veal & MaKinster, 1999). **Pedagogical content knowledge** includes an understanding of what makes learning specific topics easy or difficult; the conceptions and preconceptions that students of different ages and backgrounds bring with them to the learning of those frequently taught topics and lessons" (Aguirre & del Rosario Zavala, 2013, p. 9). Win was presented with an opportunity to grow her pedagogical content knowledge and provide room for more student discourse, more open sharing of one's thought process, and more productive struggle by gaining conceptual understanding of the math. Whether or not Win made a shift to grow in her practice or was resistant to change is unknown, but it all hinged on her ability to be open and receptive to learning and growing. What path do you think Win chose? If she chose to deepen her conceptual understanding, how might that influence the way she teaches?

## WHAT'S YOUR DOMINANT ACADEMIC IDENTITY?

Examining your academic identity from the time you were a young learner up until now will help you better understand your instructional style and who you are as a teacher. I posit that your academic identity can vary depending on the subject matter and grade level being taught. For example, a person might have a very firm academic identity in teaching third- through fifth-grade math due to their extensive continuing education in math instruction (such as additional certifications, coursework, or professional development) but also have a foundational academic identity in teaching phonics and word recognition. A teacher can have a different type of academic identity based on the subject area, grade level being taught, or a variety of other factors.

←――――――――――――――――――――――――――――――――――――――――――→

Foundational                          Forming                          Firm

A teacher with a firm academic identity exhibits actions, behaviors, and decisions in the classroom that reflect the belief that all students learn differently and that everyone can learn because everyone can think. Their teaching is centered on student thinking and promotes an asset-based approach to guide instructional decisions. The students in this teacher's classroom are active, valuable partners in the learning journey. On the contrary, a teacher with a foundational academic identity may run a compliance-oriented classroom where students are passive participants in the learning.

Here is a broad look at how we can classify the development of one's academic identity:

| TYPES OF ACADEMIC IDENTITIES | | |
| --- | --- | --- |
| FOUNDATIONAL | FORMING | FIRM |
| Positions the classroom experience for "instruction" rather than "teaching and learning"; acts as learning manager rather than learning empowerer | May or may not take a holistic approach to student engagement, focusing more on academics and less on factors such as physical, social, and emotional well-being | Uses a strengths and assets-first approach, referencing students' strengths, interests, funds of knowledge, and needs to build learning paths with students |

Now let's apply this spectrum from foundational to firm to the math teacher's classroom learning experience:

| | TYPES OF ACADEMIC IDENTITIES FOR MATH TEACHERS | | |
|---|---|---|---|
| | **FOUNDATIONAL** | **FORMING** | **FIRM** |
| Content Knowledge | Not secure in math knowledge; knows shifts (conceptual, procedural, application) in superficial manner, devoid of practice for oneself | Secure in math knowledge; might be stronger in one area of the shifts than the other: conceptual, procedural, application | Strong math knowledge; balanced strength in all three key shifts: conceptual, procedural, and application |
| Classroom Discourse T = Teacher S = Student | Typical cadence might be: T-T-T-T-T-T-S-T | Typical cadence might be: T-S-T-S-T-T-T-T | Typical cadence might be: T-S-T-T-S-S-S-S-T |
| Questioning as Discourse | Asks mostly yes/no questions of students; students rarely ask questions | Believes teacher should ask most, if not all, questions in class | Develops questions during lesson planning and is comfortable asking and being asked cognitively demanding questions |
| Instructional Planning | Plans or actions are applied to students | Students may or may not be included in planning | Responsive planning is done with students |

## REFLECTION

How would the three types of academic identities apply to the content area(s) you teach?

_____

_____

_____

_____

_____

It's important to remember that your academic identity is not fixed. Where you are on the spectrum — from foundational to firm — will vary depending on the subject matter, grade level, concept being taught, point in your career, time in your life, or myriad other factors. Moving from foundational to firm requires a shift in perspective — for example, believing that learners should be active, valuable partners in the learning journey, instead of passive participants in a factory-model, compliance-oriented, or **deficit-based** perspective. As your mindsets and beliefs shift, so will your instructional practices.

 **Teacher Commentary**

I think moving along the spectrum to a firm academic identity gives us the opportunity to let students teach us. It allows us to empathize with students, learn where our biases may be accentuated, and adjust because our identity is built on learning. When we design with the students, they can create a strong feedback loop that informs how we interact with them and encourages their engagement in learning.

# CHAPTER 2

. . . . . . . . . . . . . . . . . . . . . . . . . . . . . .

# MINDSETS

> *"No one can escape having prejudice, no matter how 'woke' they may be. The way someone becomes an ally is by recognizing their ignorance and realizing they'll never be exempt from prejudice."*
>
> —*Nina Murphy, age 16*

**MINDSETS**

I was a seventh-grade math teacher in a large, urban school district. I'd become disgruntled from the large class sizes, with up to 40 students and a limited supply of textbooks and manipulative tools to explore math concepts. I felt that, in any given day, I was adjusting my lessons to engage the wide range of academic diversity in my classes, covering math skills that spanned first through 10th grade.

I was elated to receive an offer to join the Teacher's Paradise (a fictitious name for a public school in a large, urban district). Though not an official lab school, this institution of learning was an experiment in the city. The hypothesis was that if class sizes were reduced to between 10 and 15 students, teachers were provided an extended day for paid, daily professional development (which included teacher planning and collaboration time), and students had access to the best equipment, tools, and resources, then increased student outcomes would be inevitable.

. . . . . . . . . . . . . . . . . . . . . . . . . . . . . . . . . . . . . . . . . . . . . . . . . . . . . . . . . . . . . . . . .

Image source: NWEA, 2023. Used with permission.

Like any great experiment, one must consider the variables being tested and the control used. And, of course, anything designed to improve student outcomes should take the students into consideration. The families of students in Teacher's Paradise had been rooted in the area for nearly half a century, forming a very rich and close-knit community with generations of families in housing built specifically for African Americans. By the time I began teaching there, the public housing was slated for a multiyear evacuation and demolition plan. My students knew that their families were going to be uprooted, and for older students, the future seemed uncertain and bleak. The neighborhood was rapidly gentrifying, and many of my students were being forced out of the only home they'd ever known. But the district assured us that they were working to correct a pattern of injustice. (Update: At the time of writing this book, that neighborhood has been gentrified. The school district is working with the city's public housing to lease part of the remaining housing to the school district in order to build a $120 million high school.)

The community had developed a reputation that undoubtedly caused outsiders to hold preconceived notions of the types of people who lived there—poor, Black, uneducated. In fact, when I told people that I was going to join the Teacher's Paradise, they were quick to warn me about the dangers I'd face day to day. These warnings revealed a belief that poverty was a culture and a choice. They failed to see how the community that housed Teacher's Paradise was the result of a "condition or symptom of the structural inequities built into our social and economic system" that promoted deficit thinking about our students and their academic capability (Hammond, 2015, p. 33).

I taught alongside four other teachers in my wing of the school—a white woman, two white men, and a Black man, all middle-aged with well-established careers as educators. Collectively, we taught about 75 young people. In an ideal Teacher's Paradise, this distribution would have been fertile ground for a holistic approach to learning, and with such a low student to teacher ratio, it would be easier to build a culture of high engagement and empowered students in intellectually curious spaces.

Within a few weeks at the Teacher's Paradise, I felt that my students had taken ownership of our homeroom and were really starting to trust that learning could be fun (again). My colleagues and I would greet our students in the hallways each morning and hold classroom meetings to start the day. We had processes in place that showed students we were all part of an engaged and collaborative learning team. I thought Teacher's Paradise was heaven compared to what I'd experienced before.

## EVEN PARADISE ISN'T PERFECT

I've taught and coached math in many different types of schools. I've delivered workshops in hundreds of schools across the nation. I've worked with veteran teachers, those new to the profession, and everyone in between, from the most prestigious institutions to the most underserved learning environments. I've been inside the classrooms in public and private schools, Bureau of Indian Education schools, independent Turkish schools, Hasidic Judaism schools, Afrocentric academies, Montessori—just to name a few school settings among many. Through all my experiences, I've learned one truism—no matter how good (or bad) a school is, there are always very effective and strong teachers, and to the contrary, there are always teachers who have a lot of room for growth—Teacher's Paradise included.

Families entrust their students to educators for an equitable education. Families hope and believe that teachers have "unequivocal faith in the human dignity and intellectual capabilities of their students" (Gay, 2000, p. 52). Ideally, teachers use knowledge from their lived experiences in concert with those of their students to make content accessible, engaging, and meaningful. In best-case scenarios, teachers and students are partners in learning, making it a "simultaneously personally validating, academically enriching, socially empowering, morally uplifting, and pedagogically transforming" experience (Gay, 2000, p. 273). Teachers typically have good intentions with our students, but once the classroom door closes, only the teacher and students really know what happens.

I am generally trusting of others and give them the benefit of the doubt, but something within kept me from believing in Mr. Wilson's jovial front and perpetual smiling and laughter. Then one day my suspicion was affirmed. I just so happened to walk past Mr. Wilson's math class during my break when I overheard him call our students "little monkeys and devils." I stopped dead in my tracks and was so shocked I could not move. I was visibly shaken and could not disregard the blatant disrespect toward our young people. Mr. Wilson had been on this earth for about sixty years, and I'm sure he knew about our country's history of comparing Black people to monkeys, and the scientific efforts to deem Black people as less than human, thus comparable to animals. Teacher's Paradise had a virus that was infecting our ecosystem.

## BIAS COMES WITH BAGGAGE

Calling the students monkeys and devils was a "small, seemingly innocuous, brief verbal, denigrating, and hurtful message [given] to people of color" (Hammond, 2015, p. 112). I'm really glad that I overheard this **microaggression** because although in my homeroom we had a classroom environment where every voice was affirmed and appreciated, my students never told me what Mr. Wilson had done. Students are "often reluctant to discuss their experiences, impressions, and thoughts about racial discrimination, ethnic inequities, and cultural hegemony" (Gay, 2018, p. 269). Students need a classroom environment that makes them feel valued. After all, how much appreciation and value would you feel if you were jokingly referred to by a derogatory term?

Assaults on a child's cultural identity are a threat to their academic identity. Mr. Wilson had a negative mindset about Black students that threatened the intellectual potential and esteem of our students. (At the end of this chapter, you will learn a four-step protocol to reframe an unhealthy mindset.) How might being called monkeys reshape a student's academic identity? Students may not have foresight to see its consequences on their academic identity for years to come, which is why the onus is on educators to understand its impact.

## Teacher Commentary

I would even go so far as to say that assaults on a child's cultural identity are the *destruction* of their academic identity.

What Mr. Wilson did is not uncommon in K–12 schools. In fact, at the time of writing this book, another white, male teacher at one of the top schools in the same school district as Mr. Wilson "hung a Black doll by its neck from a cord at the front of his classroom then argued with a Black colleague who was offended" (Issa, 2022). Students, teachers, families, and community members were outraged at such a blatant act of racism occurring while our nation was in the midst of a racial reckoning. Nina Murphy, a student at the school, shared this reflection on the importance of talking about racism:

> When George Floyd was murdered, I was upset. The feeling you get watching a police officer kneel on a Black man's throat isn't describable. It's like a mix of disgust, generational fear, anger, and sadness. Even though I was upset by what I saw, I wasn't surprised. When you grow up with outspoken Black parents, and when you go to a school that talks about racism, you aren't surprised when you witness extreme racism. My white classmates were allowed to talk about it in class, and they had similar sentiments. They, too, felt disgusted. However, many of them mentioned that they didn't know things like this happened a lot, or they said they didn't think there was a lot of racism left in the world. So a lot of them had a newfound zeal and inclination toward activism. I was — and still am — happy that they are learning about police brutality and racism. I've even educated some of my friends about race issues, but it shouldn't be the burden of the educated to educate.
>
> Just as a part of me was happy, another part was surprised. It was hard to fathom how a teenager, even a White teenager, could be so incredibly ignorant and blind about racism and police brutality. I can't imagine going through life without a strong understanding of

*how racism affects many aspects of life. Even if I could grasp that concept, I would never have the luxury of living my life in pure race-blind bliss. As a Black girl, I don't have the luxury or privilege of assuming racism "isn't that bad" anymore. Just as a part of me was surprised, another part was disappointed. It shouldn't take watching someone suffocate a Black man for people to realize that Black people are still oppressed.*

Source: Before the national outrage: Why young kids need to be taught about racism, Nina Murphy, https://www. nwea.org/blog/2021/beforethe-nationaloutrage-whyyoung-kidsneed-to-betaught-aboutracism/, 2021, NWEA. Used by permission.

## Teacher Commentary

Nina's story is very powerful. White people need to do better at understanding the privilege beneath the idea that they are "colorblind" and think that racism has been solved. The fact that this account comes from a Black girl in high school is a powerful way to convey these ideas.

Between 2020 and 2022 in the United States, most public-school students did not attend in-person classes but learned online. Some parents found remote learning to be useful in shielding their children from racism in the classrooms (Fernando, 2021), which was occurring with greater visibility. In fact, there seemed to be an uptick in the reporting of overt racism toward students by teachers in K–12 schools. A simple Internet search of "teacher calling student monkey" over the past year yielded these headlines in the news:

- NC teacher calls Black students 'my little monkeys'
- Black preschooler's 'monkey award' from teacher slammed by mother
- Michigan school suspends teacher for worksheet comparing Obama to monkeys
- Teacher resigns after racially 'insensitive' comment to Black students
- Racial slurs and 'monkey noises' targeted California high school cheerleaders at football game
- Riverside teacher placed on leave after mimicking Native Americans during math class
- School district sorry after students make gorilla noises at Black player

I feel like calling your students monkeys goes beyond a microaggression. That just seems like aggressive racism.

## OUR MINDSETS IMPACT OUR STUDENTS

I've used examples of microaggressions to introduce the entry point of mindsets because everything begins in our minds. My intent was to elicit an emotional response from you so that we could get to the inner-outer work of having equitable mindsets. A student's academic identity can be undermined by a teacher's **mindset** and how a teacher interacts with that student — the words they say and behaviors they exhibit. A mindset is a set of mental attitudes that determines how one will interpret and respond to situations. According to Zaretta Hammond, "When teachers frame student differences as deficits rather than assets, a microaggression is ignited for the student" (2015, p. 113).

> *"When teachers frame student differences as deficits rather than assets, a microaggression is ignited for the student."*

"Microaggressions are the subtle, everyday verbal and nonverbal slights, snubs, or insults which communicate hostile, derogatory, or negative messages to people of color based solely on their marginalized group membership" (Hammond, 2015, p. 47). Microggressions are not limited to people of color; they also show up through the lens of sexism, ageism, ableism, ethnocentrism, and sizeism — just to name a few. Microaggressions in schools show up as microassaults (misuse of power and privilege), microinsults (cultural insensitivity), or microinvalidations (nullification of students' funds of knowledge), each of which are further defined and elaborated upon by Hammond in *Culturally Responsive Teaching and the Brain*. Eschmann et al. (2020) note,

> *Research on microaggressions and discrimination finds negative effects on both mental health, including depression and anxiety (Keels et al., 2017; Nadal et al., 2014), and physical health, including rates of cardiovascular disease (Calvin et al., 2003). Other work finds that trauma resulting from racial microaggressions can have negative impacts on racial identity development, self-esteem, and relationships with others (Nadal, 2018). Some targets of microaggressions can have trouble determining whether a microaggression really occurred (Sue, 2010), while others hesitate to respond to microaggressions because they are worried how their peers might respond (Yosso et al., 2009).*

There is a large segment of our student population with more to overcome because they have multiple marginalized identities. Their need for teachers with cultural humility and raised consciousness about antiracist teaching is of utmost importance, lest we continue to perpetuate environments that stifle the academic potential of students.

> *If biased teacher expectations are directly or indirectly communicated to students, they provide precise information about educational investments that perceptions of student traits do not. . . . Biased expectations could be incorporated into students' own beliefs, thus influencing their investment decisions. This is especially concerning for disadvantaged students with little prior information on the returns to educational investments. Finally, while a teacher's perceptions reflect their current views of abilities or traits, their expectations are prone to becoming self-fulfilling prophecies. (Gershenson et al., 2016)*

## LET'S F.A.C.E. IT

In this section you will identify the facts and name the feelings that came up for you after reading the examples shared so far in this chapter. Perhaps you learned that there is historical context in the United States around Black people being referred to as monkeys (fact) and you felt uneasy and a bit conflicted because in your culture "devils" is a term of endearment (feeling). Maybe you felt that I made assumptions about you, the reader, because a certain population wasn't included in the stories in Chapter 1. Or it is possible that everything you read resonated with you because you'd seen or experienced something similar, and you feel affirmed knowing that you aren't the only one. Either way, you felt something. So let's identify those feelings.

The intent of this section is to build your emotional intelligence and help you gain more awareness of the feelings that arise as you do your equity work. We'll look at the F-A part of the F-A-C-E It reflection that I introduced in the beginning of this book:

- Facts and Feelings: Identify the facts and name the feelings that arise in you from those facts.

- Agree and Argue: State what you agree with and what you would argue against.

- Connections: Draw parallels to your own experiences.

- Epiphanies: Record your "ahas" and takeaways.

How you feel matters. Feelings that are not acknowledged or expressed can become suppressed. When we suppress feelings that are heavy and unpleasant, we risk taking on actions and behaviors that are destructive to ourselves or others. When we suppress feelings that are light and loving, we deny others the truthfulness of our humanity. Feelings matter because they bring invitations for action. When we feel tired, it is an invitation to rest. When we feel angry, it is an invitation to revisit our boundaries. When we feel grateful, it is an invitation to expand our life force. The feelings that arise when you do your equity work are invitations to act toward growth and change — for you and/or for others.

For this exercise, I want you to be honest and name the feelings that arose in you after reading the examples shared so far. If you are unable to identify a word to express how you feel, begin by asking yourself, *What stood out to me? How did I react to what I read?*

Here are specific questions to probe your thinking:

- When I called Mr. Wilson's name calling a microaggression, how did that make you feel?

- How do you respond when you hear colleagues making racist or sexist comments in school?

- How many of your students are like Nina? Why? How does that make you feel as their teacher?

- What feelings are coming up for you? Hopeless? Curious? Perplexed? Confused? Annoyed? Frustrated? Inspired? Intrigued?

| FACTS AND FEELINGS | |
|---|---|
| What were the facts and initial reactions you had to the people, situations, and/or topics covered in this chapter so far? | |
| FACTS | FEELINGS |
| | |

## Facts and Feelings Next Steps

Based on your responses in this section, what do you want to make sure the facilitator addresses when you and your team engage in professional learning?

_____

_____

_____

_____

_____

 **Teacher Commentary**

These exercises are affirming to me because I've had many of the same experiences as the teachers and as the students around low self-esteem in math, as well as difficult situations with intentional and unintentional racism with colleagues. This reflective work also leaves me uneasy. I'm wondering if any of my actions or words are slipping through the cracks around equity because it hasn't been top of mind lately. What microaggressions have I participated in? Have I been in situations where I've been too easy on people or let things go that put equity for our kids at risk? Lastly, I'm excited (and a little nervous) to dig deeper. Addressing big feelings and big topics like equity and racism are hard (but worth it).

## Agree and Argue

Doing equity work requires having hard conversations, and I want to help you be best prepared to engage in difficult dialogue. It's okay to disagree with others, including me. Our differing opinions are what help to strengthen our relationships when we seek first to understand and then to be understood. Let's help you get ready to share your point of view with clarity and compassion.

In this section, I want you to begin unpacking your equity mindset. The first step is to identify the things that you agree and disagree with in order to illuminate your values and beliefs. To define the things that are inherently important to you and the opinions you stand on, you'll identify things that sounded sensible to you in Chapter 1, as well as the things with which you disagree. The second part of unpacking your equity mindset will be exploring your academic identity later in this chapter.

| AGREE AND ARGUE | |
|---|---|
| Recall the situations, topics, and stories shared so far in this chapter. List at least five things with which you agree, and explain why you agree with that story, topic, or item shared. | |
| **I AGREE WITH** | **BECAUSE** |
| _____ | _____ |
| _____ | _____ |
| _____ | _____ |
| _____ | _____ |
| _____ | _____ |
| **REFLECT FURTHER** | |
| Who might not agree with you? Why? How would your perspectives differ? What might they say about your point of view? | |
| _____ | _____ |
| _____ | _____ |
| _____ | _____ |
| _____ | _____ |

## BECOMING AWARE OF MY BIAS

I want to take you to my first year of teaching and show you how much I needed the entry points for equity back then. For some educators, the first year of teaching is hard (yet very rewarding), and the learning curve is steep. I saw very quickly how adept students are at testing limits, a normal part of their development needed in order to learn boundaries. The first year of teaching for me was a crash course in classroom management, which was all about boundary setting. Success is relative, so finding those things that you're really good at and hinging on them is critical to your survival as a first-year teacher. Finding a few things that you do well can compensate for all the trial and error that comes from being a novice. So in my first year, I focused on what I knew best aside from teaching math, and that was how to be a girl based on my experience as a young girl navigating middle school. I saw myself in the girls in my classroom — their behaviors and ways of thinking — and as a result, I ended up paying them a lot more attention than the boys. I often called on girls a lot more than boys because I remembered what it was like to be overlooked as a young girl in math class. I was biased, and here is one way my bias showed up in my classroom:

- **A missed opportunity for equity:** I often predicted that the boys would not score as well as the girls on tests, noting that the girls had better reading skills and work habits, which would influence their scores.

- **An equitable mindset:** A colleague helped me understand that my prediction was an assumption. They helped me better understand the negative impact gender biases and stereotypes had on students' engagement and learning.

**Note: Girls and boys were gender pronouns that were socially accepted and used by society during the time of this teaching experience.**

If my prediction about student performance were backed by data, it would be less wrong, less biased, and less harmful. But it was an inequitable mindset that got in the way of me affirming the intellectual capabilities of all students. My intention was to encourage girls that I felt were at a disadvantage because of their past experiences with being looked over in math class, but the impact was that I made the boys feel invisible. I saw myself in action (through observations and videotaping) and witnessed how my behavior impacted student engagement levels. I needed to change my mindset because my bias was fueling a greater narrative of restricting access and opportunity to the boys in my classroom. When we adopt equitable practices of inclusion, we not only increase engagement among students but also strengthen our academic identities as well as those of our students.

*I needed to change my mindset because my bias was fueling a greater narrative of restricting access and opportunity to the boys in my classroom.*

## REFRAMING YOUR MINDSET

> *"Imagine being a student who is seen only through the lens of his or her deficits: as the student who can't sit still in class or disrupts class with outbursts. Now, imagine how it would feel to be that same student, yet instead you're seen as the child who has more energy than anyone else and therefore can get much more done, or as the child who smiles at everyone and is always in a good mood. This is how asset-based approaches change perspectives in the classroom."*
>
> —*Diana Turk* (NYU Steinhardt, 2022)

You might be wondering what to do if you work with a teacher like Mr. Wilson or if you notice other teachers using language or exhibiting actions and behaviors indicative of a deficit-based mindset toward students. It is important to approach any interactions with deficit-focused colleagues with the intent to learn and share, not to change anyone. Trying to change someone creates barriers to the doors to conversation that inquiry can open. Please note that while some actions and behaviors may need to be explicitly called out, particularly if they put students or fellow educators in danger, other ways of thinking should be allowed time and space to grow.

Deficit thinking refers to the idea/worldview that particular students fail in school because the students and their families have "deficits" that impede their learning (e.g., limited education, poverty, minority status).

Shifting from a deficit- to asset-focused mindset first requires a shift in perspective. Here are four simple but powerful ways to guide someone through a mindset shift. These four steps help you avoid trying to fix, change, or save students and encourage greater empathy and understanding of students' lived experiences.

### Making a Mindset Shift

1. **Name the issue.** Allow the person to articulate what the issue is and why they think it exists. It is important for the person to identify the things that they don't like, that bother them, or that are problematic from their point of view. If it's not stated or seen, then it can't be reframed.

2. **Assume good intent.** Next, explore reasons why the issue might exist, but do so from an unbiased and nonjudgmental stance. Avoid blaming

the student or feeling pity or sympathy for them. Instead, empathize with that student's lived experience. For example, if the problem was that a student is constantly disruptive in class, assume that the student wants to engage productively in class and explore the barriers that might be preventing the student from doing so.

3. **Identify the needs.** Now, step fully into the student's shoes and gain empathy for their actions and behaviors by identifying the student needs (i.e., emotional, physical, psychological, etc.) that are not being met. Explore reasons why the student reacts in certain ways when their needs are not met. What might change if those needs are met for the student? Keep in mind that a student's needs are neither good nor bad. The strategies they sometimes use to meet their needs can come across in ways that have an unexpected impact on others.

4. **Reframe the issue.** Now, revisit what was shared in step one and retell it from a more compassionate perspective, taking into account what the student needs and what actions, behaviors, and choices the teacher can make to help meet those needs.

Here is an example of an educator shifting from a deficit- to asset-focused mindset using the four steps.

## Making a Mindset Shift

| NAME THE ISSUE | ASSUME GOOD INTENT | IDENTIFY THE NEEDS | REFRAME THE ISSUE |
|---|---|---|---|
| *The parents of my lowest- performing students don't seem to care about school. They don't respond to my emails and notes.* | *Maybe there are things I don't know that explain why we aren't connecting. I am a parent. I know life gets busy and I can't make all of my kid's events, but I try my best because I want the best for my kid. Maybe my students' parents are in similar situations.* | *A community literacy specialist came to our last staff meeting and told us that an estimated 50% or more of the students' caregivers could not read beyond a third- or fourth-grade level. I realized that almost all my emails and letters home were at the eighth-grade level. No wonder I wasn't getting responses from parents!* | *My students' parents want the best for them, and I have to work to make sure I communicate in a way that is easy for them to understand.* |

# REFLECTION

What feedback would you give this teacher about their reframing?

_____

_____

_____

_____

_____

Now, apply these four steps to yourself. Think of an issue that you have had to reframe your thinking about. Complete the following table. Share your thinking with a colleague who may provide additional insight for you.

## Making a Mindset Shift

| NAME THE ISSUE | ASSUME GOOD INTENT | IDENTIFY THE NEEDS | REFRAME THE ISSUE |
|---|---|---|---|
|  |  |  |  |

## MAKING CONNECTIONS

The first two tenets of equitable and excellent education are using an asset-based mindset and setting high expectations for students, specifically the following:

**Practices of an equitable and excellent education**

1. Using an asset-based mindset
2. Setting high expectations for students
3. Offering rigorous instruction for all
4. Creating a welcoming, inclusive, and affirming environment
5. Building relationships with the community

In what ways are you upholding an equitable and excellent education for your students? The following reflection will help you assess your understanding of the intersection between mindsets, academic identities, and equity.

# REFLECTION

1. How are mindsets connected to academic identities?

_____

_____

_____

2. How are mindsets connected to equity?

_____

_____

_____

(Continued)

*(Continued)*

3. Can you think of an inequitable experience that a student experienced? In which ways was their academic identity undermined?

_____

_____

_____

# CHAPTER 3

........................................

# RELATIONSHIPS WITH EDUCATORS

*"I've got to do the personal work so I can do the professional work, which is where I get the platform to do the real work."*

—*Michael K. Williams,* Scenes From My Life

**RELATIONSHIPS**

Equity and relationships in K–12 education is a multilayered topic. Most discussions around equitable relationships center on race and cultural relevance as a focal point for dissecting how teachers relate to students. In fact, it is imperative that we talk about race — and specifically whiteness — because "white [people] are often able to live and flourish in a state of race neutrality . . . their whiteness gives them privilege, opportunity, and a naivete that shields them from what it means to have a racial identity" (Henning, 2021). A white teacher and friend of mine once said that she got offended when someone mentioned white privilege, but when that same person asked her which race or gender has the best chance of jogging alone at night, my teacher friend understood white privilege immediately. Understanding the historical contexts of race, whiteness, and white privilege and how they relate to inequities in K–12 education is essential learning, but that is not what this book is about. *The Equity Expression* helps you think

............................................................

Image source: NWEA, 2023. Used with permission.

about equity from a new perspective. In this chapter, we'll explore what it means to amplify your agency by creating your community, cultivating collaborative learning spaces, and making self-reflection a consistent part of your practice so that you can have better relationships with other educators. The big question this chapter will help answer for you is, *What can I do to continuously improve myself and my practice in ways that create an excellent and equitable education for all students?* If we want to disrupt a system, we must be willing to disrupt ourselves.

> *If we want to disrupt a system, we must be willing to disrupt ourselves.*

Today's teachers are not all the way okay: They are feeling burned out, overworked, and overwhelmed. The 2020 worldwide pandemic created an urgency to shift how we do schooling, it caused additional stress on how we live day to day, and the pace of ever-increasing politicized topics in education resulted in educators being more reactive than proactive. Teachers need the time and space to bring awareness to how they feel about these changes so that they can make empowering choices and take equitable actions in their day-to-day teaching. What do you do with the angry feelings you have about how your state has passed legislation stating that you can't discuss certain topics or issues in school? Where do you put the guilty feelings from the times your class waited outside the bathroom because there weren't enough subs to cover your break? How do you handle the feelings of fear that another student might get caught in crossfire after school? Sometimes these feelings lead us to react with behaviors that have a disempowering impact on others. So what do we do with these feelings? We raise our level of awareness about them, process them, and try to make sense of them through our relationships. This form of dialogic reflection is the main factor in the entry point of relationships.

Relationships offer us the opportunity to be more conscious of the actions, behaviors, and choices we make in order to achieve the most positive outcomes for students. In this chapter, I will introduce you to three steps for forming specific relationships that will support your equity journey:

1. Create your community
2. Cultivate collaborative learning space
3. Commit to self-reflection

## STRATEGY 1 OF 3: CREATE YOUR COMMUNITY

I recommend purposefully creating a small community of three to begin your equity work. Electing two trusted partners with whom you can process, reflect with, and make sense of your thoughts, actions, behaviors, content, and instruction will ensure support and growth along your journey of enacting equity. Talking about issues of equity can be challenging, especially when we broach topics that arouse emotion or challenge beliefs. Within this smaller community of three, you can more easily build collegial trust wherein you can rely on healthy, reflective dialogue with other teachers. In this way, you are beginning to reconceptualize your experience by using peer collaboration as form of self-directed learning and as an opportunity to "exercise agency in shaping [your] growth throughout [your] career" (Learning Forward, 2023). "Collaboration helps to build relational trust in the school building, which enables teachers to more effectively make difficult decisions" (Darling-Hammond et al., 2019). By choosing to strategically and purposefully align your learning with colleagues, you can address some of our most desired components of professional growth and development: (1) Discussing each other's experiences, frustrations, and ideas, (2) developing skills and content knowledge, and (3) planning equitable lessons and aligning on curriculum.

To best support your growth, select two different types of trusted partners: a 180- and a 360-partner, both of whom know what it's like to be a teacher, neither of whom evaluates or assesses your performance. Both 180- and 360-partners are people from which you will learn, and they will learn from you. Through honest, authentic conversations you can embrace diversity as you learn more about one another and deepen your self-awareness and develop skills in empathy. Here are the two types of partners I recommend:

**180-partner:** This colleague is a person you imagine to be 180 degrees different from you — perhaps in your upbringing, cultural experiences, or even subjects that you teach. If you teach math, your 180-partner might be an ELA teacher. The purpose of selecting a 180-partner is to engage in conversation where you will learn from the insight and experience of someone different from you.

**360-partner:** This colleague is a person you imagine to be 360 degrees similar to you because they are aligned in what you teach, your cultural experiences or background, and your interests. If you teach sixth-grade science, your 360-partner might be the eighth-grade science teacher. The purpose of selecting a 360-partner is to engage in conversation where it might be easier to converse on topics because you share common ground.

Consider what type of person would be your ideal 180- and 360-partner. Describe this person in as much detail as possible.

My ideal 180-partner:

_____

_____

_____

_____

My ideal 360-partner:

_____

_____

_____

_____

 **Teacher Commentary**

Some of my best years of teaching were when I taught middle school. My teacher team of six had a magical chemistry between us. For eight years, we worked together to establish an amazing rapport and sense of community unlike anything I'd ever experienced. I can only imagine how much more powerful our journey would have been if we focused our work around equity. Truthfully, many teachers don't get as lucky as I did to have a group of colleagues with such strong synergy. So starting with either a 180- or a 360-partner just might be the ticket! The key is not only the connectedness one experiences with a learning partner but finding the *time* to make it happen. If a community could be built around a grade-level team or a content team, with dedicated time to focus on equity topics, teachers might be more willing to buy in.

**Identifying your partner.** When you interact with other teachers, hold the intention of finding members for your community. Look over your descriptions for ideal 180- and 360-partners, and consider teachers who you already know. List the names of three people who could be your partners. Explain why you think each person would be an ideal partner. If no one comes to mind as a potential 180- or 360-partner, consider your upcoming professional development activities as opportunities to meet and connect with someone.

| 180-PARTNER | 360-PARTNER |
| --- | --- |
| Name _____<br><br>Why is this person an ideal partner? | Name _____<br><br>Why is this person an ideal partner? |
| Name _____<br><br>Why is this person an ideal partner? | Name _____<br><br>Why is this person an ideal partner? |
| Name _____<br><br>Why is this person an ideal partner? | Name _____<br><br>Why is this person an ideal partner? |

Knowing your purpose for having trusted partners and identifying the intent of your interactions are key to making these relationships worthwhile. Here are three ways to anchor your 180- and 360-partnerships, in addition to having someone to discuss topics of equity with from a different lens.

1. **Strengthen your academic identity:** Any new learning deserves your proper processing and reflecting time to consider how the information connects to your classroom instruction, and your academic identity. Your partner can help you think aloud and make sense of your new learning.

2. **Try out new strategies:** There's greater benefit when you can collaborate with a peer and see strategies in action with students. Whether through a classroom observation, watching a snippet of your teaching, or sharing a teaching experience with them, your partner can offer you feedback and input that can help you facilitate change in your practice.

3. **Stay encouraged:** Teaching is hard. And today, it's even more challenging with all of the demands on teachers, educational policies that challenge how we do schooling, and changes in the way we show up in person and online for learners. It's important to stay encouraged and your partner can be your cheerleader.

## REFLECTION

I wanted to gain insights from someone who might think about equity differently than me: a 180-partner. I envisioned a healthy debate on questions like, *Are racism and equity related? How are some people blind to the intersection of racism and equity? What stories are we willing to talk about, and which ones are we sweeping under the rug? How many hall passes can we continue to give to people who dismiss inequities?*

My goal was to learn from our conversation (but the optimist in me secretly wishes for equity naysayers to have a change of mind). I believe that everyone should be given at least one opportunity to grow and change, and a conversation can be that chance. I asked my colleagues if any among us had doubts or concerns about our equity work and the industry's focus on equity in education.

A white male peer and fellow educator volunteered to have a courageous conversation with me. After reading our dialogue, I'd like for you to determine whether we were 180- or 360-partners, and why. Our conversation was edited for clarity and details have been changed for anonymity. (This person has asked to be kept anonymous in the acknowledgments section as well.)

**Fenesha Hubbard:** Let's start with defining equity. What is equity?

**Educator colleague:** There are different aspects of equity, such as equity in terms of the academic outcomes we set for students. But at the core, equity is the idea of being just and fair. I want to ensure that students who have been mistreated or underserved get access to opportunities. Inequity happens when we give students the opportunity but with an unfair advantage. Consider honors courses, for example. If we lower the standards and expectations for students in honors classes and they excel with those lowered standards, then they are already behind in the next level of classes because they were not adequately prepared.

**FH:** Would you talk to the educator that might not see the inequity in that example?

**EC:** Sure. Sometimes we differ in terms of what we think the cause of an inequity is, and then we think differently about what the solution ought to be. We have to consider everyone's identity and their worldview because it has an impact on the ways we see problems, causes of those problems, and solutions. I think of a Spanish phrase I used to hear — pobrecito! A "pobrecito mindset" is one in which you look at a student with pity. You feel sorry for the student but you appear well-intended. You want to create an opportunity for the student to succeed so you lower the standards they are supposed to attain, and you do it out of pity for the student.

**FH:** Let's talk about pity. Where does a "pity mindset" stem from? What brings an educator to have a "pobrecito mentality" about students?

**EC:** There are some people who teach from their high horse. But I think people generally and genuinely don't want to be the gatekeeper who prevents students from passing, so their well-intended efforts to lower the bar so that students can jump with ease actually ends up disserving the students; it never stretches them to grow. There was a movie where a teacher went through Herculean efforts to get her students to be successful. She didn't lower her expectations. Instead, she put in tremendous effort to help the kids get up to where her expectations were or what she thought they were capable of.

**FH:** The way you describe Herculean efforts is the way a lot of teachers think of equity in action. The Herculean way is the equity way.

**EC:** There's a phrase that says, "If you put a good person in a weak system, the system wins every time." You see teachers put in Herculean efforts and then burn out. Instead, we need to work together strategically with our efforts. That way, the English teacher isn't doing it by themself, and the math teacher has a support system. When we do equity work, we should be on one accord with an understanding what that work looks like and how it should be executed.

**FH:** So how do we work together to address issues stemming from systemic racism?

**EC:** Worldview has a lot to do with racism. I believe that we are all explicitly valuable. I don't value people because constitutionally they have human rights. I value people because they're uniquely valuable humans. Therefore, doing anything that is hurtful or unloving against that human is an inequity. If we're going to talk about systemic racism, we need to define the system. We have unique issues caused by American slavery. But when it comes to mistreating others based on ethnicity or skin color, I wouldn't attribute that to the institutions in the United States but rather to an inherent human condition.

**FH:** The United States was built on a business model of slavery that had laws established to police Black people. It's engrained in our culture and shows up today as people literally calling the police if they perceive a person or their behavior to be threatening or inappropriate. Whether my human condition is good or bad, if I still abide by this system, then how will I ever make equitable change?

**EC:** I don't disagree with what you said about our history and the systems it has created. I believe you should love your neighbor as yourself. When I teach another human, I am loving that human.

**FH:** So long as you see them as human.

**EC:** Exactly. We have to honor the humanity in our students and see them for who they are and what they can be. I was an instructional coach for a white third-grade teacher in a predominantly white school with a sudden increase in the Hispanic student population. I noticed that the teacher always seated the Hispanic students in the back of the class. I told her that I noticed she didn't call on Hispanic students, and she told me that it was because they didn't know the answers. I needed to make sure I brought to light her assumptions about Hispanic students and set the expectation that such discriminatory behavior was not acceptable. That was a pivotal experience for me in terms of understanding the equity work we need to do. The teacher wasn't even aware of her inequities. In my worldview, lack of awareness is a human

(Continued)

*(Continued)*

heart problem. So until that human heart changes — and that's transformational work — until then, we aren't really doing equity work.

**FH:** I'm glad you were there to be a change agent for that teacher. Can you imagine what happens behind closed doors when no other educator is there to witness and call out the inequities?

**EC:** Sometimes you just have to be a leader and call a spade a spade; then make it stop. But in other situations, you have to get at the heart of the issue by, first, becoming aware of what the problem is and, second, finding the desire to change. We have to want to meet the needs of all learners.

## REFLECTION

1. Are my educator colleague and I 180- or 360-partners? Explain your thinking.

   _____

   _____

   _____

2. What might be an area of focus for our relationship, based on the brief conversation you read?

   _____

   _____

   _____

3. How did this dialogue differ from typical conversations about equity?

   _____

   _____

   _____

Below are three teacher profiles showing their beliefs, expectations, and fears as they relate to equity. As you read through each profile, consider whether this type of teacher could be your 180- or 360-partner.

## Anna Desiderio, Gifted Teacher – Beliefs

- What is the value in students applying their learning outside of the classroom? Explain.

  - I feel most proud and successful when my students can tell me how something they learned in class was useful for their day-to-day life. But those instances are few and far between. Many of my students are goal-oriented and focused on passing tests so that they can be admitted to the "right" school. I want parents to know that the learning we do in class builds life skills and helps students become critical thinkers and make connections between concepts they learn not only in my class but in other classes.

- How do you feel about culturally relevant classroom materials? Do they belong in your classroom? Why or why not? Explain it as you would to a colleague.

  - We have plenty of resources and materials that the students can relate to, but we are not seeing the increases in student growth and achievement that we would like to see. I like the culturally relevant materials and texts that we use, but I've noticed that I have to do a lot of modeling for students to help them learn how to approach the text with inquiry. Group work is the most challenging because when you have five or six students grappling with a concept they don't understand, either because of cultural differences or just new learning, they need more scaffolding. I've had to do a lot more whole-group instruction with the culturally relevant texts, but hopefully students will slowly learn how to hold each other accountable for learning, probing with questions and exploring more.

- What does it mean for someone to be an equity-empowered educator?

  - I think being equity empowered is not about what you teach but how you teach it. The most important thing is that your students are positioned for success, so an equity-empowered educator needs to do just that — put the structures, lessons, tools, and resources in place to make sure students can get what they need to learn from where they are. This means that you're not designing a one-size-fits-all approach to learning but rather building the learning in ways that meets students where they are and helps them grow. Equity-empowered educators are advocates for access to learning for everyone.

(Continued)

*(Continued)*

**Would this person be an ideal 180- or 360-partner for you? Why, or why not? What would you like to learn more about from this partner? How would this partner benefit from a relationship with you?**

_____

_____

_____

_____

_____

### Tim Golsby, High School History Teacher – Expectations

- Is it important for all students to contribute to your classroom lessons? Why, or why not?

  - Ideally, I'd like for all of my students to participate in class every day. But the reality is that I'm working with young people who have real issues. Sometimes if a student hasn't eaten, all they can focus on is the hunger. Or if they didn't get sleep the night before, then I can expect their energy levels to be lower.

- When, if ever, might it be acceptable for a student to not contribute to the classroom learning?

  - I always expect students to engage in class. But I realize that if a student has an accessibility issue, then it's my job to put the proper accommodations in place so that they can engage. But I can't do that alone. I need the support of my colleagues to make sure I fully understand what the student needs and that I have the right tools to support them. I've had some parents pull their student out of class during certain lessons because they think I'm teaching something too controversial. I really wish our administration team would make families a priority when it comes to equity. When parents are involved and informed, they are likely to be with us rather than against us.

- What is the role of equity in classroom instruction? Explain it as you would to a parent.

  ○ We're all unique, and our differences are what help us learn even more about the world. I'm teaching students not only how to be successful in class but how to be intelligent citizens. I know we all come across people we just don't understand or situations that don't make sense. But my job is to help students see the world through the lens of equity — where all voices matter and we seek to understand first, then to be understood.

- How would you describe a classroom that is equitable? Explain it as you would to a student.

  ○ The first word that comes to mind for me is safe. Safety, especially psychological safety, is really the key to having an equitable classroom. Their ideas and thoughts are affirmed and not judged or shut down. All of the students feel seen because the teacher and their classmates acknowledge them. Students are entitled to have their own opinions, and those opinions are respected even if others disagree. Students appreciate their differences and try to learn from one another. They have multiple ways and opportunities to engage in the learning. An equitable classroom has a safe and healthy environment where students are okay not knowing something because they understand that we're here to learn, so being wrong is fine as long as we're headed toward right.

**Would this person be an ideal 180- or 360-partner for you? Why, or why not? What would you like to learn more about from this partner? How would this partner benefit from a relationship with you?**

_____

_____

_____

_____

_____

**May Hu, Special Education Teacher – Fears**

- Do equity initiatives put restraints on what you can teach or how you can teach? Explain.

  ○ Right now I feel like they are putting a restraint on what I can teach because our administrators don't let us have much influence on the programs we select or the type of professional development we receive. We know best what our students need. We have too many equity initiatives right now, and it seems paralyzing. We have a lot of training and tools, but we need to know how to make effective decisions and plans. Sometimes, we just seem to get stuck in the same nonproductive conversations with our administrative team. There seem to be a lot of different opinions among staff about what components of equity are most important. I'd like to see them come into our classrooms to really observe what's working and what's not.

- How would you know for sure that your leadership team is well equipped to support you and provide direction as you enact equitable practices?

  ○ Our principal and their leadership team seem really coordinated when it comes to supporting us. They are very transparent about what types of equity training they are receiving and how they teach it back to us so that we can apply it to the classroom. They've created a system of peer mentors where we can get together and talk about the new practices and how they're working for our students. Since our administrators seem so aligned on what makes learning equitable, I feel like I can trust them to guide me in being more equity focused in the classroom.

- What might go wrong if you employ equitable teaching practices with integrity?

  ○ I already anticipate backlash from some parents because they think that equity means we're teaching their child about race and imposing our morals onto them. Granted, I'm a parent, so it makes sense to want to save moral education for the home. I think if we don't educate our parents first, we'll have serious backlash.

**Would this person be an ideal 180- or 360-partner for you? Why, or why not? What would you like to learn more about from this partner? How would this partner benefit from a relationship with you?**

_____

_____

_____

_____

_____

**Teacher Commentary**

As a former instructional coach and administrator, I'm thinking of how we can incorporate time into staff meetings to regularly meet with your 180-partner and your 360-partner. We're all so busy, so having designated times to consistently connect could be so helpful and valuable. I think the most important part of having a 180-partner or a 360-partner is that it is someone who is willing to do the work to look at your beliefs, thoughts, words, and actions in alignment with the definition and charge of equity that we're focused on. It also takes someone who is willing to be honest about it, even when it's tough and uncomfortable.

## STRATEGY 2 OF 3: CULTIVATE COLLABORATIVE LEARNING SPACE

Consider all the professional development spaces in which you gather with educator colleagues — trainings, workshops, professional learning communities (PLCs), webinars, staff and grade-level team meetings, continuing education courses, and so on. These spaces provide a continuous growth opportunity to develop skills and knowledge that will help make you a better teacher. The findings from a recent study "point towards the need for reconceptualization of 'teacher professional development' as an opportunity for the construction of a collective and satisfying interpretation of themselves-in-the-world, where teachers work together to make sense of both mundane reality and stressful teaching-related events through the co-construction of social support" (Ab Rashid, 2018).

It takes a great deal of courage and risk to participate in collaborative learning spaces alongside your peers because you don't know how your growing knowledge, opinions, self-esteem, or dignity will be impacted by people's reactions. In the classroom, you're enclosed in the safety of your pedagogical knowledge, and you are the subject matter expert guiding students on their journeys of learning. Outside of your classroom, your learning can feel full of uncertainty. It's important for you to have a collaborative learning space in the relationships with your peers that is non-threatening, where it's okay to not know something, and where all perspectives are welcome.

**Consider the possibilities:** Reimagine your relationships with fellow educators as collaborative learning spaces where you work alongside your peers to learn more about the subject(s) you teach, how to best teach it, and how to know what learners, in safe and brave spaces for equity conversations where critical thinking occurs, and new thoughts are explored. These spaces provide "built-in time for teachers to intentionally think about, receive input on, and make changes to their practice by facilitating reflection and soliciting feedback" (Darling-Hammond et al., 2017).

By creating a safe and brave collaborative learning space among your peers, it will become easier to navigate between what you know and what you are seeking to learn. In this space you want to purposefully use open discourse, questioning, noticing, and wondering, with the intent to develop new learning and perspective.

I encourage you to consider these ten additional norms for engagement that allow for courageous conversations and deeper learning, where you and colleagues agree to do the following:

1. Assume good intent
2. Seek to understand, then to be understood
3. Stay engaged through discomfort
4. Embrace silence
5. Listen without preparing to respond
6. Use "I" rather than "we" statements
7. Show nonjudgmental grace for other people's experiences
8. Accept that there may be more questions than answers
9. Expect that closure may not be reached
10. Respect the privacy of the space

 **Teacher Commentary**

An additional norm that I want to include is "ask permission to provide advice." I want to get better at asking if others want to be heard or if they want advice or insight. There are always people who will listen to others and then share unsolicited "you should . . ." statements.

I feel like teachers need to get to know each other to help live out these agreements and learn from each other. They need to learn who their colleagues are as people, their background, their history, and their family. This helps humanize us in our fast-paced and busy world where it is easy to make assumptions. It helps build empathy, rapport, and trust so we can live out these agreements and hold each other accountable to them. I feel like people always feel comfortable to chat over food. I wonder how we could create spaces where people would feel comfortable, get to know each other, so then we could dig into the hard topics like inequities in our own practices. Maybe start over food!

Note: Doing your part to create a collaborative learning environment among your peers aligns with the **InTASC standard #3:** *The teacher works with others to create environments that support individual and collaborative learning, and that encourage positive social interaction, active engagement in learning, and self motivation.*

## Activity: To What Extent Do You Nurture Collaborative Learning Spaces?

|  | I SOMETIMES... | I OFTEN ... | I ALWAYS ... |
|---|---|---|---|
| Ask colleagues to help me learn about their cultural backgrounds and differing perspectives |  |  |  |
| Cue others to help clarify expectations for collaborating and engaging in dialogue with one another |  |  |  |
| Use my colleagues' ideas to develop collaborative learning norms for respectful interaction, full engagement, and individual responsibility |  |  |  |

# REFLECTION

1. What does it mean to you to nurture collaborative learning spaces with colleagues?

_____

_____

_____

2. What are the benefits? What are your apprehensions?

_____

_____

_____

3. What tools or resources do you need to continuously nurture collaborative learning spaces?

_____

_____

_____

4. What kind of behaviors, characteristics, and/or skills support a group to develop a collaborative learning space?

_____

_____

_____

Reflection-focused dialogue is a key component of a collaborative learning space. Reflective practice flourishes when people experience a high level of psychological safety and trust, and it is undermined when people feel exposed to unfair negative criticism and when they believe that they cannot rely on colleagues (Chasara, 2016).

Everyone in the space needs to feel safe, especially when discussing highly charged topics around equity. "Psychological safety does not happen automatically. Because our brains are hardwired to keep us safe, our default mode is to presume some level of threat in most environments" (Gube, 2022). Here are some tips to do your part in creating a psychologically safe space:

1. **Slow down:** To digest information at your own pace, honoring your needs for processing.

2. **Speed up or extend:** Give yourself permission to engage more deeply at the pace that work best for you.

3. **Prepare to reflect:** To make the most out of your collaborative learning time with peers, set aside time to reflect on the experience either alone or with a trusted partner.

**Teacher Pro-Tip**

I want my admin team to go through these exercises so that this process can evolve organically, without a sense of "top-down." I don't often get support from my school or district admin, so that makes my work a struggle.

## STRATEGY 3 OF 3: COMMIT TO SELF-REFLECTION

We've looked at relationships with your colleagues. Now let's consider the most important relationship you will ever have: the one with yourself. It's easy to define a relationship between you and others because it's usually driven by roles (I teach my students), agreements (the building service worker cleans my classroom at the end of each day), or commonalities (we're the science team). The relationship with yourself is defined by the extent to which you are true to who you are and your willingness to grow and change. It's important that you're clear about who you are, what you believe, and your impact on the relationships you have with others. The relationship you have with yourself affects others as much as it affects you.

The entry point for equity in relationships requires self-awareness — how you see yourself and your impact on others, which can be gained through self-reflection. Self-awareness "is being aware of how consistent (or inconsistent) our self-view is compared to an external appraisal — how other people see us or against objective data" (Gube, 2022). By developing a greater self-awareness around how you view equity, you will be able to better understand the differing perspectives we all bring to the equity conversation.

Becoming more self-aware is hard. There's a myth that as educators we're more knowledgeable and more evolved than the average person; that we're the sage on stage, in the front of the classroom holding all of the knowledge that we transfer to students while being adept at discerning what students know and need to know. As teachers, we are expected to become masters of the subjects we teach and highly skilled at classroom management. However, no one explicitly challenges us to expound our social, cultural, and political dimensions of learning so that we can help our students learn the content with greater context. We must always be students of life, constantly learning and growing so that we can elevate our young people to new heights of thinking and knowing. The onus is on us to "view learning as having intellectual, academic, personal, social, ethical, and political dimensions, all of which are developed in concert with one another" because "academic success is a nonnegotiable goal for everyone and the responsibility of all participants in the teaching–learning process" (Gay, 2000).

Self-reflection requires honesty and humility. Sometimes you aren't aware of your true feelings about a thing until you experience it and have to react or respond. Please commit to being open and straightforward with yourself and about yourself when you engage in self-reflection. No one will judge your responses because they are just for you. You're safe within yourself. If your inner critic surfaces and you begin to judge yourself, consider that an invitation to be humble. Humility means accepting the fact that there are areas in which you can still learn and grow. Remember, you are doing equity work and inner work for the greater good of our students.

There are no right or wrong answers to the upcoming reflection questions. Respond without imposing moralistic judgments on yourself and don't worry about what someone else might say in response to your answers. The responses to your questions can affirm or invalidate how you feel about yourself as an equity-empowered educator. Your answers do not determine if you are a true equity-empowered educator. Engaging in this self-reflection work can help you better articulate your thoughts and ideas with your colleagues and heighten your self-awareness around equity. The conversations you have around equity will be difficult, but with your added authenticity and proper facilitation, the conversations can be structured toward change.

## DISRUPT YOUR INNER DIALOGUE

*"Action without reflection leads to burn out. Reflection without action leads to cynicism."*

—*Albert Einstein*

I once heard that if you aim to disrupt inequities, you must be willing to disrupt yourself. The purpose of this section is for you to become clear on your stance and determine what is important to you as it relates to equity, as well as to further gauge your readiness to engage in equity conversations humbly and confidently with colleagues.

Here are some thoughts from fellow educators about the three steps presented in this chapter that will add to your thinking:

 **Teacher Commentary**

▶ I wonder how to make these connections because I'm surrounded by colleagues who are exhausted, pessimistic, and angry.

▶ Needing peer support is huge for relationships. It may be hard to ask another teacher to be their partner, especially if the school doesn't find value in these connections. This comment is coming from my own experience of being told I needed a mentor. I always felt weird asking someone if they would meet with me and mentor me. Building peer support can be hard, depending on the culture of the school and the teacher. Ways to mitigate this? Maybe teachers can be encouraged to ask questions and respond to others' questions. This could help create that partnership they need. Or a peer support group or comment box where people could elect to go or submit comments? Or utilize the professional development opportunities that are provided.

▶ I think some teachers may find their 180-partners can drain their energy. If I pick a 180-partner who has yet to acknowledge the historical role of racism in education, I could become frustrated feeling that I have to constantly educate my partner. These conversations are important to have, but boundaries and my energy must be protected. I also wonder if building relationships with colleagues can help how students perceive their experience at school. If teachers have better relationships, perhaps our morale would increase and trickle down to students and their perceptions of the school environment.

▶ I feel like I've had lots of 360-partners but the idea of 180-partners is super interesting to me. I completely see the value. I'm wondering how to broach finding and building a relationship with a 180-partner. It's easy to build relationships with people that are close to you in your building or that you may plan with. I'm wondering how I would find my 180-partner.

▶ I present as white and have visible privilege; therefore, I often think about how I demonstrate my care about this topic. I don't think it's equitable for people of color to take all of the responsibility for equity work. Folks who are "othered" in their identities don't always feel they belong to the conversation. This reflection opens the door to conversations with consideration of

(Continued)

*(Continued)*

yourself — do you care about this topic? Do you think it's relevant? If yes, then you are centering on equity.

▶ I truly do believe that I'm equity empowered in my thoughts and beliefs. Being honest to myself about my actions and how they play out consciously or unconsciously is the hardest part. It takes focus to really examine even the smallest of actions like nicknames for students to ensure that my actions align with beliefs.

▶ I've had relationships with 360-partners that seemed to elevate my own teaching. We were able to learn from each other and challenge each other. You might make a mistake, or you may learn something new. That's okay, though, because this journey is not about getting to perfect; it's about doing better over and over again. It's about continuous learning. It's about being able to notice barriers and then break them down.

Reflect on the following questions related to forming relationships with your colleagues and peers.

## UNCOVER YOUR BELIEFS

1. What do you believe to be true about forming relationships with people we call 180- and 360-partners?
2. What does it mean for someone to be an equity-empowered educator?

## EXPRESS YOUR EXPECTATIONS

1. What feelings have come up for you when you think about creating and cultivating your relationships in an intentional, planned manner?
2. Is it important for all students to contribute to your classroom lessons? Why, or why not?

## FACE YOUR FEARS

1. Do you feel any resistance to the idea of being an equity-empowered educator? Why?
2. How would you know for sure that your leadership team is well equipped to support you and provide direction as you enact equitable practices?

## SUMMARY

Teaching is hard work. I doubt I would have thrived during my teaching career without the community I created and cultivated. I formed connections with my grade-level team members. I engaged with my mentor and instructional coach at least once a week. And I found clarity within myself by making self-reflection a regular practice. Each of these relationships were reflective in nature. They gave me the space to **consciously complain** and try to make sense of all that I had to manage as a teacher, particularly things that pained me or that I found challenging. Talking my thoughts out helped me to identify my feelings so that I could teach from a space of clarity and confidence, rather than confusion.

The people in these relationships were witnesses to my teaching journey, hearing and seeing my point of view and offering a different perspective. They helped me "return to my experiences and attend to how I felt about them" so that I could "examine more closely, give meaning to my experiences, and think more deeply and holistically about issues, leading me toward greater insights and learning" (Serrat, 2013). This type of support ensured that I returned to my love of teaching. Without these relationships, I could have easily let untended feelings fester into resentment, pessimism, anxiety, frustration, or exhaustion. This community gave me what I needed to thrive as a teacher and affirmed my work. They were able to say, "I see you. I hear you. Without judgment. And here's what I see. Here's what I hear." My community helped me make connections between my thoughts, challenges, ideas, and beliefs. This reflective dialogue helped me figure out what to do with my feelings, showed me that my thoughts and reactions to happenings within the education system were normal, and gave me the clarity and confidence to enact my own agency.

My community was heterogeneous. Although I taught math, I made sure to connect with teachers in other subjects because we taught the same students. I also needed to connect with other Black women educators to affirm and help me make sense of my experiences (am I the only one on staff that keeps getting asked questions about my hair?). These teacher types were always part of my community. I also made a concerted effort to connect with educators that didn't teach middle-grades math and didn't identify as a Black woman. Connecting with a variety of teachers also showed me the different ways inequitable systems can be physically, mentally, and emotionally taxing. This helped me see how systems of oppression are navigated differently through subject-matter content and teacher demographics. You need a community to help you make sense of the thoughts, beliefs, ideas, and experiences that you have about issues of equity.

## Teacher Commentary

▶ In order to be a true champion of equity in our schools, we need to self-reflect deeply and honestly but also find a community of people who are willing to do the same for you.

▶ 180- and 360-degree partners will help each of us to see how we can become better teachers. The relationship we have with ourselves and our commitment to inner change shapes who we are as teachers.

▶ This chapter built on the work we started in the first two chapters and gives actionable steps you can take to strengthen your relationship within your school community and with yourself. We now have tools to set up a collaborative community.

# CHAPTER 4

......................................

# RELATIONSHIPS WITH STUDENTS

> *"You never really understand a person until you consider things from [their] point of view—until you climb into [their] skin and walk around in it."*
>
> —*Atticus Finch,* To Kill a Mockingbird

**RELATIONSHIPS**

Relationships are an essential part of the equity expression. We are here to learn and grow from one another, whether our perspectives are similar or different. The previous chapter focused on the relationships with yourself and fellow educators because having healthy and authentic relationships with one another can make it easier for us to work together to help our students learn and grow. Relationships with students are equally important because we teach students, not just content. Students are young people that really do want to learn and grow, although sometimes their actions and behavior communicate otherwise. I believe that part of learning and growing is trying new things and testing your limits. And isn't this what young people do best? Our job as educators is to accept this truth about students and

.....................................................................

Image source: NWEA, 2023. Used with permission.

provide the guidance and guard rails along their journey. Sometimes the guardrails are rules; other times they are advice. Equity comes into play when they inform the rules and advice that we provide young people to help them learn and grow. Making equitable decisions for someone requires that we have some insight and understanding into that person's perspective. So let's hear from the young people.

A group of eighth graders were asked questions about what works and doesn't work in building relationships with students. The questions focus on inclusive practices of acknowledging students' presence, honoring the sweetest sound to them (their name being called), and making them feel welcome. I wanted to get the student perspective on microinsults that they might experience, such as when a teacher doesn't learn how to pronounce a student's name or gives them a nickname to make it easier for the teacher (Hammond, 2015, p. 113). Imagine one of your students as you read the responses. This visualization will personify the student voices for you.

**Have you ever felt ignored or invisible in class? Why? What would you want your teacher to know?**

- Yes. I want my teacher to know that when I have seizures, I can't be surrounded.

- Yes. When I raise my hand and the teacher won't even look my way. I want them to know I am smart and pay attention in class. I am willing to learn.

- Yes, they have ignored me when I've asked questions to help me understand the work. If they ignore me for too long, I'll just walk out because I might as well not be there.

- Yes, when my teachers treat everybody the same.

**How does it feel when teachers mispronounce your name? What do you want teachers to know?**

- I feel kind of offended. It's okay to get it wrong the first time. After the first time, I feel like you doing it on purpose.

- It makes me feel like my name is very different from everyone else.

- When teachers mispronounce my name, I don't respond. They should say my last name first, and then ask how to pronounce my name.

- Irritating because it always happens.

- I feel disrespected. Approach me in a way that you'd like to be approached.

- Annoyed.

**What do you wish teachers did to make you feel more welcome in class?**

- Come to school with a good vibe.

- I wish that the teachers would greet us with a handshake or something.

- Get to know us more. Talk with me about my day.

- As long as we are doing the work and following along, we shouldn't always have to raise our hands and speak because some students don't like the attention of being called on.

- Let us express ourselves more.

- Be more open instead of just assuming things.

- Say good morning to everyone.

- Bring a positive, energizing attitude.

- Motivate me by giving me kind words.

- Let us relax sometimes.

*Students are experts at a lot of things that teachers aren't, and the classroom should be a place where learning happens with both the students and the teachers.*

# REFLECTION

1. Which of the student responses affirm things that you already do with learners?

   _____

   _____

   _____

2. Do any of the responses make you feel uncomfortable or defensive, either because you've lost a good habit of practice or because you know that you could do better in a particular area? Explain.

   _____

   _____

   _____

3. How might you respond to the students who answered these questions?

   _____

   _____

   _____

## CULTURALLY RESPONSIVE CONNECTIONS

We must talk about how to employ equity in the classroom because not all of us understand what it means for "academic success to be a nonnegotiable goal for everyone and the responsibility of all participants in the teaching–learning process" (Gay, 2000). Some educators identify the intersection of equity, teaching, and learning as culturally responsive teaching, culturally sustaining pedagogy, antiracist teaching, social justice, etc. — just to name a few of the validating and affirming practices that require bringing students' funds of knowledge into the learning experience.

The common thread through these ways of teaching and learning is good teaching that honors the humanity of our students and recognizes that students' lived experiences are worthy enough to connect to the content we teach. I dare to say that all teachers want to connect with their students, but many among us do not know how to identify with our young people, or have "beliefs about ethnic, racial, social, and cultural diversity" (Gay, 2000, p. 23) that are "ambivalent or problematic," or they are not willing to put forth the effort to understand the students we teach.

## Cultural Relevancy

Zaretta Hammond best explains cultural relevancy by distinguishing between the tangible expressions of culture (dress, food, holidays) and the foundations of culture (worldview, group values, core beliefs). Hammond defines collectivism and individualism as the **cultural archetypes** that influence how we engage learners, noting that these archetypes exist on a continuum. Features of individualism include competitiveness, self-reliance, and independence. Collectivism has characteristics that are more collaborative and relational, with a focus on group interaction and success. "Some cultures are individualistic with little or no collectivistic elements, while others might be primarily collectivistic with strong elements of individualism. It is simply a starting point for building on the shared culture of your students" (Hammond, 2015, p. 26).

I once facilitated a workshop for a group of teachers in a rural town of Wyoming. During our break, one of the teachers pulled me aside and said, "I really love this workshop! You're so professional and engaging. I love your hair too! I was wondering if you could help me with an issue in my classroom. I have a new student and she's the only Black girl in class. Would you give me some tips on how to engage her more in class?" A doleful smile painted my face. I felt the full burden of being the Black woman responsible for teaching non-Black women how to relate to Black students. But a shift in perspective allowed me to see that this teacher genuinely wanted to help her student. She felt safe enough to ask for help on how to make the learning relevant to the student's culture. She didn't want to make the young Black girl's funds of knowledge an afterthought.

 **Teacher Commentary**

I'm a white teacher, and I've had many white teachers tell me that they are afraid to do or say the wrong thing, even though they genuinely want to respect and connect with students.

On the other hand, there was Mr. Ferguson, my white male colleague who made very few attempts to connect with his all-Black class of second graders. People walking by his classroom likely heard him yelling at his students on any given day. By the time the dismissal bell rang, his tie had become undone and hair disheveled. Mr. Ferguson struggled to establish rapport with his students: a group of eager-to-learn seven-year-olds who just wanted to show their teacher how smart they were and to gain his love and approval in return. It was obvious to the students that Mr. Ferguson felt like he was from a different world and couldn't relate to his students' lives. One day, Mr. Ferguson's mentor candidly told him that he needed to care about the students as if they were his own. His mentor suggested that he spend time in the neighborhood, frequenting places where his students would go — the YMCA, the local library. After spending time in the community alongside his students, Mr. Ferguson began to see a different side of his students and noticed how much they responded to interaction, music, and movement. The textbooks Mr. Ferguson used didn't suggest adding these components to the lessons, but by doing so, students were much more captivated by the learning. He practiced what Geneva Gay calls culturally responsive caring by "acquiring knowledge of and accepting responsibility for culturally diverse students that go beyond the school day and its organizational parameters" (Gay, 2000, p. 62). Mr. Ferguson enhanced his instructional style so that the students learned in a way that was relevant to their collectivist cultural archetype.

Connecting the content to a topic in ways that interest students can make it easier for you to engage everyone in the learning. However, interest alone doesn't suffice for meeting a learner's academic needs. Varied assessment options must be included so that students can show their understanding in different ways that made sense to them. This is a subtle but impactful way to build rapport with students because it shows that how they learn matters to you as their teacher. It affirms their ways of thinking and doing.

## REFLECTION

Let's identify the insights from this chapter that will inspire more meaningful relationships with students.

List three "aha's" that you got after reading and processing this chapter:

1. _____

2. _____

3. _____

List two main ideas from this chapter that you want to explore more:

1. _____

2. _____

List one thing from this chapter that was new learning for you:

1. _____

## FURTHER READING

For additional support on how to develop relationships with students, I recommend Chapters 5 and 6 of Zaretta Hammond's *Culturally Responsive Teaching and the Brain*. Chapter 5 focuses on "Building the Foundation of Learning Partnerships" for effective student–teacher relationships, and Chapter 6, "Establishing Alliance in the Learning Partnership," "explores the special stance and skills teachers need in order to leverage relationships and culture" with students (2015, p. 8).

 **Teacher Pro-Tips**

Here are some pro tips from students about how to build better relationships with them:

▶ Believe that we are good.

▶ Be more understanding of our feelings.

▶ Share information about your life with students and ask students about their lives.

▶ Respect my personal space.

▶ Don't pressure students to do something they don't want to do.

▶ You don't always have to raise your voice all the time.

▶ Listen to me. Be there when I need you. Take up for me. Spend time with me.

▶ Try to not be so hard on us and understand we are trying every day.

▶ Make us feel welcome.

(Continued)

*(Continued)*

- ▶ Don't try to fit in with us, but be there and be one-on-one with us.

- ▶ Be sincere.

- ▶ Engage with your students in a positive way.

- ▶ Don't be so serious all the time.

- ▶ Give us reasons to smile.

- ▶ Be more understanding and patient.

- ▶ Pull students to the side and ask them if they are okay if they are not behaving right.

- ▶ Do classroom bonding activities in the beginning of class.

- ▶ I like incentive systems that tell me exactly what to do and what I'll get for doing it.

- ▶ Try your best to understand and hear us instead of instantly saying, "No."

- ▶ You need to be understanding.

- ▶ Try to be more fun, not just on Fridays.

- ▶ Talk more with students individually because everyone isn't the same. Treat your students with respect.

- ▶ Make the work fun.

- ▶ Have fun; don't be so hard on us.

- ▶ Just try to be nice.

- ▶ Be a fun teacher that likes to play learning games.

- ▶ Reward us after we do good.

- ▶ Be more understanding. We are kids, and we have feelings too. Respect goes both ways.

# CHAPTER 5

....................................

# PRODUCTS

*"If you believe something doesn't exist, you don't go looking for it. Worse, if you stumble on it, you still can't see it."*

—*Dr. Rebecca Hall,* Wake

**PRODUCTS**

In the previous chapters, we did a lot of inner work. We looked at academic identities, mindsets, and relationships as they relate to equity. The work you completed so far may have felt like therapy. You had to go within to explore your beliefs and ideas. You did what Geneva Gay calls *practicing possibilities*, in which "educators need to be explicit and transparent about the ethics and ideologies that anchor their culturally responsive practices" (Gay, 2000, p. 53). When you practice possibilities in this way, you are taking the beginning steps in "converting ideological claims and beliefs into behaviors"(2000, pp. 53–54). In this chapter, we'll focus on the entry point of products and key considerations that help you enact equity with tools for learning.

We've defined equity as the fair treatment, access, opportunity, and advancement for students that facilitate their individual success and belonging. Equity is what eliminates the barriers that put students at a disadvantage. Equity is important because all students deserve to have an opportunity at academic success. One way we give students opportunities is by ensuring

..................................................................

Image source: NWEA, 2023. Used with permission.

they have access to high-quality, intellectually challenging, appropriate content. In this chapter, we will look at the guiding principles for selecting products and the ways you can build your capacity for using products for equitable teaching. The main question this chapter will help you answer is, *Am I teaching students what they need to learn in a way that is of a high academic standard and addresses the intellectual, academic, personal, social, ethical, and political dimensions of equity?* Through a series of self-assessments and reflections, we will look at what it means for a product to be equitable, identify ways that product use can do harm to students, and examine the two main components of equitable products: student partnership and product experience. The work in this chapter will be enhanced if you continue the discussion with your team of educators. If you are completing this work in a group setting (which I recommend), it's best to approach the chapter in segments in order to better focus your discussions.

Making teaching and learning equitable takes a concerted effort to use products that support you in eliciting "student thinking in ways that recognize and embrace their humanity" (Guarino et al., 2022, p. 405). You have to understand not only who your students are and what they are ready to learn but also what matters to them and what composes their many identities. Before we begin the work of this chapter, reflect on your thoughts about products and equity.

## REFLECTION

1. What do you believe is important about products used by students?

   _____

   _____

   _____

2. Why is it important to ensure that the products we use are equitable for students?

   _____

   _____

   _____

3. What do you believe is important about products for teaching and learning?

_____

_____

_____

4. Why is it important to include products that are relevant and meaningful to students?

_____

_____

_____

5. How can learning about your students' academic identities help you choose the right products?

_____

_____

_____

## PRODUCT PURPOSE AND INTENT

Products are tools used by students in the teaching and learning process that provide learning opportunities for students (i.e., learn new content, learn about how you learn as a student) and teachers (i.e., learn what your students know and what they are ready to learn, learn about how your students learn best). These tools that enhance our teaching and student learning can include curricula, textbooks, novels, manipulative tools, software, assessments, electronic devices, and more. Before you continue reading, pause and list at least ten types of products you use with students:

1.

2.

3.

4.

5.

(Continued)

6.

7.

8.

9.

10.

Review your list and identify three products you use most frequently with students. Assess the purpose and intent of those three products by answering the following questions:

- What kind of information about your students do these products generate?

  _____

  _____

  _____

- What do your products reveal about student learning?

  _____

  _____

  _____

- Do the products on your list give students an opportunity to learn content? To learn about how they learn? To learn what they know? In what ways?

  _____

  _____

  _____

- When using the products, how can students demonstrate what they know?

  _____

  _____

  _____

- Which of the products on your list require student input, such as completing a task that shows their understanding?

_____

_____

_____

- How many of your products are a one-way means of receiving information, such as a book of poems or instructional video?

_____

_____

_____

- How do these products support your instructional choices?

_____

_____

_____

- What is the purpose of the products you use?

_____

_____

_____

## High-Quality Instructional Products

High-quality instructional products and materials, when used effectively, can improve student achievement. At the very least, products are tools that do three things: (1) help students learn, (2) show you how students learn, and (3) give you information (data) that helps you decide where to go next in the learning. Products are equitable for young people when they have the following qualities:

- student-centered
- support a learner empowerer model

- support a culture of learning
- involve a high level of student partnership
- allow for formative assessment by teachers
- offer an accessible experience

These characteristics are not the sole determinants for an equitable product, but they are essential.

Equitable product use should entail using the tool for **formative assessment** — a planned, ongoing process used to elicit evidence of student learning to improve student understanding of intended disciplinary learning outcomes and support students to become self-directed learners. Formative-assessment strategies, practices, and tools inform instruction and help move learning forward.

Sometimes a lack of purpose and intent with product use will leave you data-rich and information-poor. For example, have any of these points ever resonated with you?

- I have too many products and supplemental tools.
- I have a lot of opportunities to make the use of our products more equitable, but I don't know how to prioritize.
- Even though I strive to make our product use equitable, I don't know if I'm missing something.
- I am making our products culturally relevant for students, but I don't seem to see greater engagement in the learning.
- It's overwhelming to feel like I'm supposed to make every single product equitable for each and every student.

## Product Overload

Product overload can lead to analysis paralysis in which you have so much information to inform instruction that you don't know what to do with the information or how to prioritize data so that it helps guide your teaching. You might be very intentional in making products culturally relevant to students, finding ways to connect the content to your students' lives, or engaging students in the content in ways that honor their culture, only to wonder if you're doing enough or too much. Feeling overwhelmed and uncertain can be the result of a simple misalignment in which what you believe to be true about instructional materials doesn't match up with what you're actually doing with the materials.

## Belief Versus Reality

Let's examine what you believe to be true about the products you use and the current reality of how you are using the products. Complete the "Belief Versus Reality" table, referring to your list of ten products as a reference.

## Products: Belief Versus Reality

| BELIEF: TO WHAT EXTENT ARE THE PURPOSES OF PRODUCTS YOU USE LISTED BELOW CRITICAL TO YOUR WORK? | | | | | PURPOSE OF PRODUCTS | REALITY: HOW OFTEN ARE YOU CURRENTLY USING THE PRODUCTS FOR THE PURPOSES LISTED BELOW? | | | | |
|---|---|---|---|---|---|---|---|---|---|---|
| NOT IMPORTANT | | | CRITICAL | | | NEVER | OCCASIONALLY | | | OFTEN |
| 1 | 2 | 3 | 4 | 5 | | 1 | 2 | 3 | 4 | 5 |
| | | | | | **INDIVIDUAL STUDENT** | | | | | |
| | | | | | Assess student readiness | | | | | |
| | | | | | Identify students for special programs | | | | | |
| | | | | | Demonstrate how student learns best or prefers to learn | | | | | |
| | | | | | Shows what students know and are ready to learn | | | | | |
| | | | | | Student self-assessment for reflection and continuous improvement | | | | | |
| | | | | | Student goal setting | | | | | |

(Continued)

*(Continued)*

| BELIEF: TO WHAT EXTENT ARE THE PURPOSES OF PRODUCTS YOU USE LISTED BELOW CRITICAL TO YOUR WORK? | | | | | PURPOSE OF PRODUCTS | REALITY: HOW OFTEN ARE YOU CURRENTLY USING THE PRODUCTS FOR THE PURPOSES LISTED BELOW? | | | | |
|---|---|---|---|---|---|---|---|---|---|---|
| NOT IMPORTANT | | | CRITICAL | | | NEVER | OCCASIONALLY | | | OFTEN |
| 1 | 2 | 3 | 4 | 5 | | 1 | 2 | 3 | 4 | 5 |
| | | | | | **TEACHER/ CLASSROOM** | | | | | |
| | | | | | Create instructional focus for individuals and groups | | | | | |
| | | | | | Lead goal-setting for individuals and groups of students | | | | | |
| | | | | | Grouping/ regrouping students for instruction within the class | | | | | |
| | | | | | Differentiate instruction within the class | | | | | |
| | | | | | Scaffold instruction within the class | | | | | |
| | | | | | Collect evidence of student learning | | | | | |
| | | | | | Collect evidence of student learning to assign grades | | | | | |
| | | | | | Teacher self-assessment and reflection | | | | | |
| | | | | | Compliance | | | | | |

Source: Comprehensive Assessment Survey APA ©2017 Northwest Evaluation Association. Used with permission.

# REFLECTION

Capture your responses to the following questions, which will stimulate your thinking about products that you use for teaching and learning.

- What do you notice about your responses?

  _____

  _____

  _____

- Are there gaps between what you believe and what you practice?

  _____

  _____

  _____

- Where does there need to be greater alignment between purpose and intent of the products used by students in your classroom?

  _____

  _____

  _____

- Describe your ideal product for teaching and learning. Prioritize the purposes of the product in order of importance to you.

  _____

  _____

  _____

Below are teacher reflections on products. Review their responses to see what you agree with and what you might argue with, and capture your reply in the space provided.

| TEACHER COMMENT | AGREE | ARGUE |
|---|---|---|
| There are gaps between what I believe and what I practice. I feel like I need to work with my team for accountability, ideas, and splitting up the work. It is hard to go at these alone and even process them alone. I know with more minds saying the ideas and beliefs to people, I'll be more accountable to ensure my actions reflect my beliefs. | | |
| I'd like to have more choice in the products purchased by my school and district. | | |
| Our team teacher said he wasn't going to have students read a certain novel because he didn't want any backlash from families. It seems that the teacher's decision was based on fear and it makes me wonder how many teachers are reconsidering the products they use in the classroom. I wonder how many of teachers' decisions are based on vocal parent groups rather than on the kids. | | |
| Talking about products is where many teachers may feel stuck because they are given products from the district that they have to use, and those products might not be equitable. I remember having to teach *Of Mice and Men*. Luckily, our curriculum team asked us to select supplemental materials (such as articles and pictures) that would help students better understand what life was like for African Americans during that time period. However, I took it a step further and prepared students for the blatant racist words | | |

| TEACHER COMMENT | AGREE | ARGUE |
|---|---|---|
| and actions toward the book's Black character. I allowed space for students to discuss how reading the words and images made them feel. That led to a deeper discussion on what it means for students to read many "canonical" texts with such horrible imagery. | | |
| My team received a lot of push back when we used social justice materials with our students. But we continued to introduce these resources, which were embedded in the Social Justice Standards. We used a rubric to evaluate if the critical elements of diversity and justice existed in the materials. Over time, as more teachers became interested, we made it a standard to vet new products using the rubric. That process truly helped teachers elevate their awareness of the importance of having products in which students could see themselves. | | |
| I believe that our students, just like everyone else, deserve to see themselves in the classroom curriculum and values. We need to show our effort and love for them so they understand that we value them. Rita Pierson says, "Kids can't learn from teachers they don't like." I think they probably could, but I like the point Rita is trying to make: It's not easy. It's easier to learn from teachers they like, and although they don't need to be your friend, they need to know that you're rooting for them, you care about them, and you value them. Incorporating them — our students — into the products of our teaching and learning helps them know that you're on their side. I believe learning should be fun, engaging, relevant, and interesting. | | |

| TEACHER COMMENT | AGREE | ARGUE |
|---|---|---|
| Incorporating our students' backgrounds and interests in the products of our teaching makes learning fun and keeps kids coming back for more! | | |
| Culturally relevant classroom materials are so much a part of my classroom that they aren't seen as added components to the classroom or curriculum. Students are seeing themselves and others through the literature we read as a class and in their independent reading choices. The materials help us have open and honest conversations about how the content connects with our lived experiences. | | |

## STUDENT AND TEACHER ROLES

Students should have a role in the products that you use to support their learning so that they are not solely users of the product. A learner empowerer mindset is the perspective that learners are active, valuable partners in the learning journey (instead of passive participants in a factory-model, compliance-oriented, or deficit-based perspective). When mindset shifts about products from a learner manager model to a learner empowerer model, products can become tools for equity.

Teachers have the responsibility to enhance students' product experience. Using products with an equity focus means teachers and students work together to make effective use of products in a way that they inform instruction, empower the learner, meet students where they are, and guide them toward higher academic standards. It also means that teachers are intentional about finding opportunities to address the intellectual, academic, personal, social, ethical, and political dimensions in ways that make either the content or how the content is learned relevant to students' lives and applicable to a context greater than the classroom.

Here are key questions for teachers and students to answer prior to using a product and to assess the level of equity that the product initiates for teaching and learning.

| | TEACHERS | STUDENTS |
|---|---|---|
| Informing instruction | • What information about my students from this product will I use to inform instruction? How?<br><br>• What information will this product give about my students that helps me know how to enhance their product use? | • What am I being asked to learn?<br><br>• What am I being asked to show that I know?<br><br>• Why am I showing what I learned in this way?<br><br>• What other ways can I show what I know? |
| Learner empowerment | • What modifications might be needed so that this product is accessible to all students? | • What's working for me with this product? What's not working?<br><br>• How do I know if I'm successful with this product? |
| Academic rigor | • How will I set learning goals with my students for this product?<br><br>• How does the product address unfinished learning?<br><br>• How can the product support unfinished teaching? | • Where am I now? Where am I going? How will I get there? |
| Success criterion | • What does success look like for students across the academic continuum using this product? | • How do I know if I'm successful after using this product? |
| Dimensions of equity | • How does the product foster learning and stimulate intellectual curiosity?<br><br>• How might I adjust my teaching and learning to complement the cultural references in the product?<br><br>• In what ways does the product support me in connecting students' home and school experiences? | • How does this product help me grow as a student?<br><br>• How does this product support the different learning styles of me and my peers? |

(Continued)

*(Continued)*

| | TEACHERS | STUDENTS |
|---|---|---|
| Potential for inequities | • Does the product overuse a narrative that renders my students invisible? Can students see themselves in the product?<br><br>• Does anyone plan to use student data from this product for tracking or another high-stakes purpose? (This matters only if the product is not intended for these purposes.)<br><br>• Is this product designed from a dominant cultural perspective that assesses for privilege or language, rather than content? | • Do I see myself in this product?<br><br>• Do the assessment questions seem too hard to understand? (Is there potential for the product to assess interpreting something rather than assessing understanding of the content?) |

## An Instructional Coach's Reflection

I recommend that teachers set aside specific times during the school year to engage with these questions with their peers. However, making it a habit of constantly asking these types of questions about all of the products you use will help the questioning becoming second nature to you, and that is the goal.

## AIMING FOR EQUITABLE PRODUCT USE

The following continuum will help you assess your current and desired use of equitable products in your learning environment. I recommend that you discuss your ratings with team members that can help you ideate solutions.

### Where Are You Now?

Rate your current use of products based on the criteria listed in each category.

| CONTINUUM OF PRODUCT SELECTION AND USE | | | |
|---|---|---|---|
| **UNALIGNED** | **EXPLORING** | **DEVELOPING** | **ACCOMPLISHED** |
| • Reviewed and shared among grade-level team members<br><br>• Teachers may or may not modify instructional strategies based on review | • Reviewed and shared among grade-level team members and staff, identifying strengths and needs<br><br>• Teachers are encouraged to work together to discuss specific instructional strategies to employ based on review | • Formal process is in place among teachers to review on a regular basis<br><br>• Strengths and needs are identified and communicated to staff<br><br>• Grade-level teams and/or PLCs regularly discuss and analyze student work | • Process of collaborative inquiry is used in reviewing products on a regular basis<br><br>• Strengths and needs are identified, and action plans are created based on the reviews<br><br>• Consistent monitoring of product use, student achievement; adjust action plans accordingly |

## Where Are You Growing?

Make a plan of action to move forward on the **Continuum of Product Selection and Use** by answering the questions listed.

- **Goal:** What is something you want to accomplish with students that will be enhanced with equity-focused products?

- **Challenges:** What is a potential barrier or challenge to meeting this goal?

- **Resources:** What tools/resources have you gathered that might help you meet this goal?

- **Action Items:** What action is needed to implement this plan to meet your goal? When will you have it completed?

▶ Teachers must be intentional with the products they use in class. If they are not intentional, then it is probably not meeting the needs of all students. Sometimes it feels overwhelming to analyze all of the products I use in my teaching just for the sake of equity. But at least now I have a very specific way to start assessing whether or not the products are useful, relevant, and appropriate for my students.

▶ In order to provide an equitable education, the products used must be equitable. This requires that students have a role in the products they use in the classroom, giving them agency and ownership over their own learning. You may be overwhelmed by all the products you have to use and worry about how to make them equitable, but you just need to start somewhere and keep going; don't think you have to do everything all at once.

## FURTHER READING

To learn more about connecting students' home and school experiences through your use of products, I recommend that you explore the writings and teachings from pioneers of this work, Geneva Gay and Gloria Ladson-Billings. Their work addresses the role of cultural competence, critical consciousness, and diversity in teaching and learning.

# CHAPTER 6

........................................

# PROCESSES

**PROCESSES**

This book has helped you think about equity from a different perspective, and the entry point of processes offers an opportunity to challenge what you've been taught about assessments, and reframe how you think about assessment processes in teaching and learning. All of our teaching and learning processes hinge on assessment, where we gather information and data about what students know. This includes assessment processes, such as formative assessment (gathering evidence of what learners know and can do), responding to that evidence together, and certifying that learning has taken place (summative assessment). Students and educators thrive when these processes stay focused on learner context, academic goals, and partnership.

We can use assessment processes to help learners grow. We gather data that inform teaching and learning, to ascertain a student's level of readiness, and to provide feedback that moves the learner forward. In order to best help a learner grow, it's important to partner with them to (1) know and understand their context, (2) examine their learning goals, and (3) use

........................................
Image source: NWEA, 2023. Used with permission.

that context and goal information to engage in teaching and learning processes together.

Think about the types of information that would help you answer the following questions about one of your students:

1. **How do we elicit learning evidence?** Identifying current knowledge and unfinished learning requires that we use assessment for learning — we assess, then we learn what the student knows, we assess again, and we learn more about what the student knows. This is referred to as **assessment for learning,** or what we think of as **formative assessment** — an ongoing process used to elicit and use evidence of student learning to improve student understanding. Since students are always learning and growing, our answer to the question *how do we elicit learning evidence* will include preplanned actions and in-the-moment moves.

2. **How do we certify learning?** What are the larger learning goals? The focus here is often on content standards. Academic goals or expectations are generally set by national and local standards, which are assessed using tests *after* learning, to determine what the student knows and at which academic level they perform. This is referred to as **assessment of learning,** where we determine how a student performs against intended disciplinary learning outcomes.

Too often, assessment for learning (formative assessment) and assessment of learning (summative assessment) are done *to* or *for* students. When we "do" teaching, learning, or assessment processes *to* or *for* students, we can miss opportunities to include student voices and identities. We can miss opportunities to amplify their agency as learners. We can make decisions based on assumptions or biases, which can create learning barriers and disempower learners.

Components that are critical for equity include (1) broadening our definition of success to include more than academic achievement, (2) embedding assessment processes into teaching and learning processes as one fluid journey, and (3) co-owning processes with students throughout this journey. These equitable moves are what we call assessment *as* learning.

Through assessment as learning, assessment processes propel student motivation, inspiration, agency, and success because they have active and meaningful roles and responsibilities throughout the learning journey in ways that value students' identities and increase achievement. Here's one way to see the differences as well as the overlaps among the three frames:

| KEY QUESTION | HOW DO WE ELICIT EVIDENCE OF LEARNING? | HOW DO WE CERTIFY LEARNING? | HOW DO WE GET THERE TOGETHER? |
|---|---|---|---|
| Frame | Assessment *for* learning | Assessment *of* learning | Assessment *as* learning |
| How it occurs | Assessment first, then learning | Learning first, then assessment | Assessment occurs while learning |
| Purpose | Formative assessment | Summative assessment | Formative, summative, and more |
| Definition | Formative assessment is a planned, ongoing process used by all students and teachers during learning and teaching to elicit and use evidence of student learning to improve student understanding of intended disciplinary learning outcomes and support students to become self-directed learners. | Processes used to certify learning, often at the end of a set of lessons, unit, or course. In contrast with formative assessment, summative processes are evaluative in nature and may help make determinations in grading, reporting, placement, and improvement in teaching and learning. | Assessment processes are embedded, fluid components of teaching and learning accomplished *with* students as partners throughout the learning journey to propel academic achievement, well-being, and self-efficacy. |

Source: NWEA. (2022) Responsive Learning Cycles Glossary

Note: Researchers from across the nation and internationally define assessment as learning in different ways.

Students and educators can have better teaching and learning experiences when assessment is a co-owned process informed by learner context to attain more than just academic success. Assessment as learning is a frame that can help us realize our goals for educational equity.

## ASSESSMENT AS LEARNING

To better understand how **assessment as learning** can be applied *with* learners to enact equity in our classrooms, I sat down with a responsive teaching and learning and quality classroom assessment expert, Erin Beard, M.Ed, D.Ed. Erin Beard's dissertation explored the intersection of assessment, equity, and trauma-informed practices. Her answers have been edited for clarity.

## Why Do We Need to Rethink Assessments?

We need to make sure we're partnering with colleagues, students, and families to regularly pause and ask, (1) What is the purpose of the selected assessment process and tools that we use? (2) What are we planning to do with the results? (3) Does the assessment and its purpose fit the context, the chosen outcome, and its placement in the learning progression? and (4) do our uses of the assessment process, tool, and results match the purpose they were designed to serve?

## How Would You Explain *Assessment as Learning* to Teachers?

In my professional journey, I learned about formative assessment, what we're calling *assessment for learning*, and summative assessment, which is what we're calling *assessment of learning*. These are the types of assessment processes I was trained in as a teacher. Eventually, I began to notice a disconnect between how we taught and what we assessed, as well as a greater disconnect from the other parts of teaching and learning. Assessment as learning connects all of the processes — and not just for academic success. It's also connected to student well-being and self-efficacy. Assessment as learning gives us a more fluid and human-centered view of and approach to teaching and learning processes, including assessment and data use. We can include our students in this fluidity so that assessment and data use don't feel like it is something that interrupted learning or was being done *to* learners, but rather it is an integral part of the teaching and learning process that is accomplished *with* learners.

## Why Is Assessment an Equity Issue?

Our nation has an outdated narrative of the teaching and learning process, including assessment. It's what I experienced as a student and how I was trained as a teacher. In this model, there's a pattern of teach, then test, then grade. In this model, academic success can be overemphasized at the expense of other kinds of important learning and success, such as well-being and self-efficacy. Assessments and data can be used as "gotchas" or even weapons against students and educators rather than opportunities to show knowledge and skills. This approach can be detrimental to our students and educators, especially those who have experienced toxic stress or trauma, which can include historical, racial, and adverse childhood experiences. In other words, the outdated model can create barriers to learning and even retraumatize people. We want to prevent and mend that. There can be a conscious or unconscious mindset that students are empty vessels that need to be filled or fixed, which is a deficit-based perspective. Not everyone succeeds in this model, but that was acceptable for a long time; in fact, ranking, sorting, and not everyone making it was considered a sign that the class, course, unit, lesson, quiz, or test was tough enough. For a very long time, this model was widely expected and accepted. But it's one reason why we have educational disparities, and why we should really consider *assessment as learning*.

## What Does This Look Like From a Student Perspective?

Here's an example of assessment as learning in action: Instead of playing a math game for games' sake or as a "break" from learning, my learners and I used the game in assessment as learning processes — one that generated all kinds of information, data, and learning evidence that we could use for responsive next steps that supported whole-human learning inclusive of their academic, social, emotional, physical, and agency needs. This entailed four simple steps:

1. **Review learner goals and context.** We reviewed the large learning goals, which for us included the content standard as well as our class agreements for physical, social, and emotional safety; individual responsibility for learning, and teamwork. We discussed how engaging in the game process helped us build toward success with those large goals. This included making connections between the large goals, the paths to get there, and students' interests and aspirations.

2. **Observe how we learn.** We observed each other during the game, and afterward, we discussed questions to help us learn about how we learned — questions such as, Were we guessing? Peeking over the shoulder of our table partner? Rapid answering? Why? Which questions were easy? Which ones need more review? What were our results? Were we able to keep hands and feet to ourselves? Did we keep voice volume to a reasonable level so as not to interrupt learning in other classrooms?

3. **Co-plan next steps.** We captured our observations about those questions and collectively made responsive next steps. Sometimes we did this formally, in writing, or informally with verbal debriefs. The intent was to summarize what we observed and use that summary to make individual and group next steps that moved the learning forward — not just academic learning but well-being and self-efficacy too. That might look like having "review stations" and "extension stations" set up the next day so that some students could do more review of the concepts while others could explore from a different perspective or in greater depth. Some students noticed that the game was too stressful, so we crafted a new version of the game together, and they used that the next day during station time.

4. **Rinse and repeat.** We repeated those steps as needed, increasing students' responsibility in the process as we progressed. Eventually, there was enough evidence that the learners were ready for assessment-as-learning processes that got beyond content knowledge and into skills

and take the next steps with what would support well-being and self-efficacy. Then, we would engage in assessment-as-learning processes to move forward in responsive ways.

## How Did This Example of Assessment as Learning Promote Student Agency and Success?

Assessment serves as a process that promotes student agency and success when there's a learner empowerer mindset. This means that we see that the purpose of the educator and learner having time together is to propel academic success, well-being, and agency, **not** to manage, fix, or fill students with knowledge, march them through content, or make them comply.

The assessment-as-learning process revealed important information about whole-human success, not just academics. Here's what I saw evidence of:

1. **Student ownership.** The responsibility of crafting and leading the learning process was not entirely on my shoulders, which was a relief!

2. **Greater purpose.** Students didn't ask "Is this for a grade?" or "Does this count?" or "Why do we have to do this?" They could see that yes, the game is fun, but it's not just busy work. It wasn't seen as a delightful escape from learning or a painful assessment experience. The game and the process of engaging in the game was helping them to work toward the larger learning goal in a fun yet deliberate way.

3. **No surprises.** We made small, doable responsive moves throughout the learning journey so that when it came time for larger assessment processes, like the chapter test or summative assessment for the learning goal, students were set up for success. There wasn't a need for big, surprising, or scary moves — akin to when students feel stumped by test questions because they don't reflect the learning experience. Overall, the students' summative scores and end-of-quarter grade data were positive. I also saw this performance among my students who qualified for SPED and EL services because we could make responsive in-the-moment actions as needed before little things became too big or overwhelming.

Although it seems like this process can take up a lot of time, it's important that we reframe it as a reinvestment of time. Instead of a cycle where we teach, then test, then grade, and then get frustrated and exhausted by failing grades and "problem" behaviors, we maximized the game and assessment process as learning to get the most out of it — academically, socially, emotionally, physically, and with increased self-efficacy. With practice, learners get the hang of the process and can do more of it themselves even when using other tools.

Assessment as learning also ensures that the social, emotional, and physical aspects and impacts of teaching and learning, including assessment, are balanced and integrated with academic aspects and impacts.

## So How Do We Shift Toward the Assessment-as-Learning Process?

We first have to understand the importance of shifting our language in a way that invites students to engage with us as partners in teaching and learning. Identifying the key terms that need to be reframed, then applying those changes in our day-to-day instruction in order to engage students will help us move toward the assessment-as-learning process. When learners can make their own meaning and connections for our assessment processes, they are more likely to engage.

## How Does This Shift in Language Relate to the Learner Empower Mindset That You Mentioned Earlier?

Think of the components of teaching and learning: there's the formal and informal — the tangible things we see such as grades and scores, and the intangible things inside, the human-centered components. A lot of times educators are good at implementing the tangible but not as effective in the human-centered components. The few educators who can successfully implement both are what researchers call *learner empowerers*. It's a shift that takes time, but I believe that the way education is shifting makes it a lot easier for us to all become learner empowerers.

## How Do We Inspire Students to Shift Their Thinking Around Assessments as Learning?

Repositioning our mindset toward human-centered practices with students helps shift the narrative about assessments. Sometimes, educators might think they have to pile on social-emotional, equity, and trauma-informed training and practices on top of everything else they do, and this can feel exhausting! But when we put this counternarrative and shift in thinking into action, we partner *with* our students. This means we use their learner context as an asset in teaching and learning, which interrupts a factory-model, learner manager way of thinking and doing actions *to* students. Shifting our thinking around assessments as learning for students takes us away from the assumptions, biases, deficits, and beliefs that can create learning barriers, that can take away learning opportunities, and that can traumatize or retraumatize students. Shifting toward assessment as learning makes it easier for educators to employ the best of human-centered, equity-informed practices.

*"Assessment isn't a stand-alone thing. When we remember that teaching and learning are full of all sorts of processes, including assessment processes, we can remember to partner with our students before, during, and after the test, quiz, or product. Then, the actions we take are informed by them, making the learning journey far more meaningful, relevant, and positively impactful."*

—*Erin Beard, M.Ed, D.Ed,*
Student-Centered Assessment Literacy

# REFLECTION

Reflect on my interview with Dr. Beard, listing thoughts and ideas that you might want to address with other educators.

| What squares with my thinking? | What is swirling in my mind? |
|---|---|
| | |

| What is challenging to me? | What do I need or want to understand? |
|---|---|
| | |

## MAKING THE SHIFT HAPPEN

Changing your perception of something requires that you look at it differently. Expanding our definition of assessment to include assessment as learning requires shifts in mindsets and changes in the words we use when talking about assessment, so let's start with key terms we frequently use: teachers, students, instruction, gaps, assessment / test, classroom, and data. These words describe *what* and *who*. In the next section we will explore the *why* and *how*.

Take 5–10 minutes to brainstorm and articulate what you know and what you wonder about these key terms. You'll have time to revisit the learn (L) column later in the chapter.

### Key Terms: K-W-L Chart

|  | WHAT I KNOW | WHAT I THINK I KNOW | WHAT I WANT TO LEARN |
|---|---|---|---|
| Teacher |  |  |  |
| Student |  |  |  |
| Instruction |  |  |  |
| Assessment / test |  |  |  |
| Classroom |  |  |  |
| Data |  |  |  |

Shifting the language that we use helps us create an asset-based, forward-thinking, and responsive counternarrative to inform our assessment processes and data conversations. In these shifts of language, along with using assessment as learning, students (or, learners) naturally become our partners in the teaching and learning experience. They become more self-aware agents of their process and progress because the assessment as learning process ensures that learners understand what they're learning (e.g., the purpose, the connection to other content), how they are learning it (e.g., what helps them learn best, how they know they're learning), and why they are learning (e.g., connections to an academic goal).

To expand our view of these terms, let's consider the *why* and *how*. Examine the suggested reframing of the basic terms and capture your immediate responses using the reflection questions.

## Reframing Key Terms

| SHIFT FROM | SHIFT TO | RATIONALE |
| --- | --- | --- |
| Teacher | Educator | It takes the collaboration of many educational professionals to make impactful and meaningful learning experiences for students. Taking an integrated approach to teaching and learning requires collective work and responsibility. |
| Student | Learner | To support our young people in attaining their full potential as thriving individuals with healthy academic identities and agency, we acknowledge that students are more than just recipients of knowledge; they are co-owners of their learning. |
| Instruction | Teaching and learning | Teaching and learning is a holistic perspective to the process we engage in with students that accounts for the intellectual, academic, personal, cultural, and social dimensions that learners bring to the learning environment. |
| Student strengths and needs | Learner context | Choosing to see beyond students' unfinished or underdeveloped learning means taking into account their strengths, needs, interests, funds of knowledge, and identities (i.e., learner context), all of which compose their learning journey. In this way, learners are seen as assets in the teaching and learning process. |
| Assessment/ test | Assessment process | Assessment processes, practices, and tools are integrated into teaching and learning. Cycles of "teach, test, assign grades or scores" don't automatically assume that learners will be empowered by the process or that they will be intrinsically motivated to perform well. Assessment processes that include the learner in understanding what they are learning and why, provide them with a roadmap for how to attain their learning goals, and assess their progress help to build relationships for growth and self-efficacy. |
| Classroom | Learning environment | Educators who create psychologically safe spaces and nurture a collaborative classroom culture are better positioned to foster the growth of healthy academic identities with a learning-focused environment. |
| Data: Learner manager | Data: Learner empowerer | Learners are active, valuable partners in the learning journey, rather than passive participants in a compliance-oriented perspective. Instead of using quantitative data to manage what we do to students, let's take a human-centered approach to using both quantitative and qualitative data to empower learners. |

# REFLECTION

Reflect on these language shifts using the prompts below:

1. What squares with your thinking? What do you disagree with?

_____

_____

_____

2. What are some ways that the old language (i.e., "shift from") can be harmful?

_____

_____

_____

3. When might the term "teaching and learning" be more appropriate than "instruction"?

_____

_____

_____

4. When might the term "instruction" be more fitting than "teaching and learning"?

_____

_____

_____

5. What types of data typically inform your teaching and learning?

_____

_____

_____

(Continued)

6.  How do these language shifts empower students and educators to co-own teaching and learning?

    _____

    _____

    _____

7.  What are the possible benefits of an integrated and collaborative approach to assessment processes?

    _____

    _____

    _____

8.  How would you explain the assets-first approach to using the term *learner context* instead of using words like *gaps* or *deficits*?

    _____

    _____

    _____

9.  What are some ways that you might gather, understand, and use students' context to inform assessment processes that fuel learners and learning?

    _____

    _____

    _____

10. In what ways has this reframing challenged or shifted your thinking?

    _____

    _____

    _____

Read how Mrs. Awasthi, an eighth-grade math teacher, used the mindset shift from assessment as a test to assessment as a process to empower her students.

> *"I changed my practice to regularly collect qualitative data on student context. I changed how we start class each day by talking about math we were learning and why it was tricky or difficult. There's a daily wall calendar to show what teaching and learning looks like: Is this an exploration day? Peer review day? Test day? We discuss how each assessment event has formative and summative parts — the formative to make sure you can swim in the deep end of our math pool. Learners can delay a test event if they need more practice swimming. Clarifying the learning path this way daily does take up class time, but it's useful time. In fact, student participation has slowly gone up and my kiddos see that it's okay not to get it right all the time and that asking for help is a good thing. A big lesson for me was that some of my students' zone of proximal development is mismatched with the curriculum map and they need instructional supports. But the real barrier for some of my students is anxiety related to learning and demonstrating math learning. The process of clarifying the learning path and calling out anxiety barriers helps to get students regulated and enables them to fully access more parts of their brain that otherwise may be occupied by anxiety. It also allows for students that are frequently disengaged to come in, get regulated, and participate. When I compare my curriculum map pace from this year to last year (during the height of COVID), we are further along and doing more advanced math this year. This new approach has armed my students with agency because it provides them with time, space, and talking points to advocate for their academic and social-emotional needs."*
>
> *—Dalia Awasthi, 2022–23 academic year*

Mrs. Awasthi made data collection on student context a regular part of her practice. She used assessment as a process to gather evidence of her students' understanding (formative assessment) and used it to inform teaching and learning. Mrs. Awasthi noticed that her assessment processes empowered students so that they took a vested interest and active role in their learning. Using data productively created a learning environment fueled by intrinsic motivation among her learners. Mrs. Awasthi was an "assessment-empowered and equity-focused educator who effectively used data by being mindful about assessment while aligning all decisions to the assessment purpose."

I used to conduct reading and writing conferences with students to ask, "How's it going?" Students would begin to talk about their learning instead of a summary of work. Hearing students teach me what they knew about the content was powerful! It was easy to let them see how their response to my simple question showed how invested they were in themselves in the learning process. Students knew they held the reins.

Many teachers are just like Mrs. Awasthi — finding relevant and useful ways to make assessment processes and data tools to empower their students. They use data to understand the learner holistically, making equitable choices that celebrate growth alongside proficiency. They understand how nonacademic factors such as houselessness or homelessness, poverty, high-stress trauma, and byproducts of systemic racism can put students at a disadvantage, resulting in lower performances on assessments, so they adjust accordingly. In what ways are you putting equity in action through assessment and data processes?

**Reflect and Connect:** Consider the approaches used by Mrs. Awasthi and identify things you want to incorporate into your practice, or refine by indicating whether it is new to you (N), you knew about it already (K), you already apply it when possible (A), or it is fully integrated into your practice (I). Include additional thoughts you have about each category, such as things you wonder about or want to learn more about.

| STRATEGIES | TEACHING AND LEARNING | OPPORTUNITIES |
|---|---|---|
| Advocate for multidimensional ways of thinking and doing among students | Use an asset-based approach to teaching and learning, where the learner context is a critical component of the process | Use assessment for learning to help students be more motivated and create opportunities for students to grow |
| Rating (circle one): N K A I | Rating (circle one): N K A I | Rating (circle one): N K A I |

| STRATEGIES | TEACHING AND LEARNING | OPPORTUNITIES |
|---|---|---|
| Encourage ways of thinking, habits of thinking, and ways of doing among students | Make learning plans and instructional moves in partnership with students (instead of plans or actions applied *to* or *for* students based on assumptions or outdated information) | Use assessment as learning, helping students become more aware of their thought processes, how they learn, and how they feel about the learning |
| Rating (circle one): N  K  A  I | Rating (circle one): N  K  A  I | Rating (circle one): N  K  A  I |

Code: N = new to me, K = knew about already, A = apply when possible, I = is integrated into my practice

*When we use data to improve our practice and support student outcomes, we can build bridges to success.*

## LET'S RETHINK ASSESSMENT AS LEARNING

The three key takeaways so far from this chapter are:

1. The assessment processes we employ can be equity in action — how we create more fair and academically rigorous learning experiences for all of our students.

2. Attending to the purpose of our assessments will help us ensure an alignment between the learner context and learning goals.

3. Examining our assessment processes helps us unpack the assumptions, biases, and inequitable decisions in our practice.

## REFLECTION

*Got it!* – What do you understand about what you read?

*Need it!* – What do you need to move forward in your learning about what you read?

(Continued)

(Continued)

|  | GOT IT! | NEED IT! |
| --- | --- | --- |
| Using learning-goal-aligned assessment processes for different purposes (e.g., formative, summative, interim) |  |  |
| Incorporating students and families into the assessment process |  |  |
| Aligning assessment processes with learning goals |  |  |
| Helping students monitor their learning, understanding, feelings, and progress |  |  |

**Further reflection:** Revisit the K-W-L chart that you completed earlier in this chapter, and add additional information based on what you have read thus far.

## ASSESSMENT EMPOWERMENT PRINCIPLES

You've learned the essential elements of assessment empowerment in this chapter. Assessment serves as a process to promote student agency and success when educators and learners work together to apply the five assessment empowerment principles. These principles help us shift from a *learner manager* to a *learner empowerer* mindset.

### Assessment Empowerment Principles

1. Analyze and apply learner context.

2. Cultivate a community of learning.

3. Attend to assessment purpose.

4. Engage in responsive learning cycles.

5. Exchange learning evidence information.

Now, let's apply these principles to a student named William, whose story is told by his teacher. Read William's story through the lens of assessment empowerment and consider ways to enhance his teaching and learning experiences.

> *William is a very confident student who shows a great capacity to learn math. He demonstrates abstract ways of thinking about math and concrete ways of doing math. William verbally articulates his solutions to math problems with ease, and he was very open and receptive to learning about how other students solved the same problem differently. He is usually the first to raise his hand and participate in our classroom math discussions, where productive struggle is the norm and everyone is encouraged to grapple collectively with their thoughts and ideas.*

Yesterday during class, we were interrupted by an argument between William and Shawn. Shawn had discovered something about William and brought it to his attention. The realization made William very angry, and he welled up with shame. Defending his honor at that moment was all that mattered. William lashed out at Shawn, yelling as he jumped out of his seat, and started pacing the room with fists balled at his side and a head hung low. I know that anger comes to remind us that one of our boundaries has been crossed.

Shawn discovered that William could barely read. Seventh-grade students typically know how to read text at their grade level. But in William's school district, only 21% of seventh graders can read at grade level. Over the years, William has become an expert at creating boundaries to shield his illiteracy. I've seen him memorize the chart of key vocabulary terms posted on the wall and identify words from sight when they appear in a different context. William deflects when he is asked to read by posing open-ended questions to me and his classmates. He gets help from peers to read a piece of text or write anything to submit for a grade.

William had fallen behind a long time ago and never caught up. Now he's in seventh grade, and I want him to feel empowered. He's felt shame for so long because he doesn't know how to read. William feels "less-than" his peers, and I want to help him reframe the disempowering feelings of shame into empowering emotions to help him grow in new behaviors and healthier habits.

# REFLECTION

1. What stands out to you about William and his teacher's description?

_____

_____

_____

2. How would you design William's learning environment to make it psychologically safe?

_____

_____

_____

(Continued)

*(Continued)*

3. How might William become actively involved in managing his learning and instructional time?

_____

_____

_____

4. How might William's teacher support his learner context?

_____

_____

_____

5. Devise a large learning goal that can be set with William. Use as much description as possible.

_____

_____

_____

6. What additional context information about William can help inform how his teacher supports him in reaching this larger goal?

_____

_____

_____

7. What might an *assessment-as-learning* experience look like for William?

_____

_____

_____

I had a student very similar to William many years ago. The good news is that I shifted my focus to relationship building and not compliance. I designed his learning environment to feel safe. I actively found ways to connect with him and better understand his reality. William's confidence grew to the point where he was demonstrating grade-level work. His overall engagement in school increased. William was so proud that he went out of his way to thank me by making a customized sports pillow because he knew I was a huge sports fan! I still have that pillow!

## STUDENT VOICES ON ASSESSMENT

I spoke with teachers and students to get insight into their understanding of the role of assessment processes in their schooling. A teacher shared that it's her "responsibility to connect students' scores to their day-to-day learning in the classroom so that they can have more ownership of their learning." The students were then asked, "What advice would you give to your teachers about how to use assessments in a way that is helpful to you?" Here are suggestions from eighth graders on how to make their assessment processes better:

- Sometimes students need a break.
- Give us more time because everybody doesn't work at the same pace.
- I need another way to try to show what I know.
- Talk about our data after school or in private.
- Help me explain my thinking.

Image source: iStock.com/Ali Kahfi

- Give us study guides so we're not caught off guard.
- We need more brain breaks.
- Make me feel good when I do work.
- Sometimes I want a cheat sheet.

## REFLECTION

1. What might your students say if they were asked how to improve their assessment processes?

   _____

   _____

   _____

2. What steps can you take to embrace *assessment as learning* with your students?

   _____

   _____

   _____

3. How can you help students better understand their role in the assessment process?

   _____

   _____

   _____

*"When I was a new teacher, the buzzy emphasis was on formative versus summative assessment. As I dove into this concept of student-centered assessment, I wondered, Is it new? Is it different? Is it an approach? Is it a mindset? And I'll freely admit, I had to battle a bit of teacher buzzword fatigue, a reality in this profession. Yet I went on a little mind connection journey that helped me buy in. First, I believe that growth matters. Second, I believe that growth is relative — and different for everyone. Third, if I'm to foster my learners' growth, I need to measure where they are and how it's going. Finally, I must center my learners in that measure of growth."*

—*Erin Beard, M.Ed, D.Ed,*
Student-Centered Assessment Literacy

## FURTHER READING

For more information on equity related to assessment as a product, I recommend *Grading for Equity* by Joe Feldman. To learn more about student-centered assessment, check out the following: Myron Dueck's *Giving Students a Say*, Jan Chappuis's *Seven Strategies of Assessment for Learning*, Hattie, Fisher, and Frey's *Developing Assessment-Capable Visible Learners, Grades K–12,* and Zaretta Hammond's *Culturally Responsive Teaching and the Brain.*

# CHAPTER 7

· · · · · · · · · · · · · · · · · · · · · · · · · · · · ·

# SPACES

*"Motivation to learn is fostered for learners of all ages when they perceive the school or learning environment is a place where they belong and when the environment promotes their sense of agency and purpose."*

—How People Learn II: Learners, Contexts, and Cultures

**SPACES**

A well-designed classroom is a gift to your learners! You know the excitement you get setting up your learning environment at the start of each school year? Let's build on that excitement by adding equitable purpose and intent. In this chapter, we'll explore what it means to create a teaching and learning space that allows for intellectual curiosity among students and why that is an equitable move.

Schools are like ecosystems, and each classroom helps build the overall environment and culture of a school. An equitable learning environment has high-functional spaces for students that are set up in a way that makes sense for the learning that will take place.

A space is an area allocated for a particular purpose. Spaces set the stage for certain activities, impact our mood, and influence our actions and behaviors. For example, playground spaces provide room to run around and play

· · · · · · · · · · · · · · · · · · · · · · · · · · · · · · · · · · · · · · · · · · · · · · · · · · · · · · · · · · · · · · · · · · · · · · · · · · · · · · · ·

Image source: NWEA, 2023. Used with permission.

games, making users of the space healthier. People frequent coffee shop spaces because the atmosphere is conducive for socializing, working independently, and grabbing a snack. Coffee shops can be energizing. But if you started running around a coffee shop playing the game *I Spy* or handball against a wall of Roger J. Carter art, you would be kindly asked to leave because that conduct is not aligned to the intended purpose of the space.

Spaces for teaching and learning should be designed to allow learners to engage without constraints. I recall a time when I was delivering a workshop for teachers and there was only one adult-sized seat in the room. It probably didn't matter how engaging my session was or how eager people were to learn — it's hard to grasp the concepts of SEL when your back is in pain and your bottom is losing circulation from sitting so low to the ground! I once was assigned to work in an unoccupied janitor's closet when I was a math coach. There were no windows in the space, and the room doubled as storage for old textbooks. I'm certain that mice were my officemates, though they worked after hours. My dignity would not allow me to work in that room because anything created in a janitor's closet would be infused with the messages that space conveyed to me: *You don't need or deserve anything better than this to do the work of servicing our teachers.* Instead, I chose to meet with teachers in their classrooms. Working together in spaces that conveyed messages of learning aligned with my intention to help teachers learn and grow. (Teachers deserve proper spaces, too.)

Think about the last work-related space you were in before you started reading this chapter (e.g., teacher's lounge, your homeroom, auditorium). Describe the space. What did it look like? Sound like? Feel like? Smell like? What did you instinctively want to do in that space? Did you want to stay in the space? Why or why not?

The entry point of spaces opens up a dialogue about how to change the makeup of our learning environments to foster and protect intellectually safe spaces for students' curiosity to thrive. Now, consider the last space your students visited in your learning environment. How would they describe the space? From their perspective, what does the space look like? Sound like? Feel like? Smell like? What is the purpose of the space? What did students do in that space? Were the students' actions and behaviors aligned to the intended purpose of the space? Take 5 to 10 minutes to capture your responses.

_____

_____

_____

_____

_____

**A note about virtual learning:** I recognize and acknowledge that the COVID-19 pandemic led to online learning and more virtual classrooms. However, this chapter focuses on physical, in-person learning environments. The reflection questions can be applied to virtual learning spaces. Teaching and learning online take a very concerted effort because you want to ensure the same level of psychological safety and engagement that exists in the in-person environment. Our brains work differently when we learn online, and for that reason, I recommend that you stay current on best practices, learn from successful virtual online learning classrooms and schools, and keep your students' needs at the forefront of all decision making.

## WHAT IS YOUR SPACE SAYING?

I'll never forget the first time my students learned science in an *actual* science lab — a state-of-the-art space with extra tall windows welcoming natural light, which was rare in our public school district. Science experiments came alive in the lab! The walls were decorated with posters of inventors, and throughout the room were plants and animals, inspiring students to grow and create. This was quite contrary to the experience my students used to have in our homeroom science class, devoid of things that orient your mind to science like lab equipment and a demonstration table. The young people were excited to go to the real science lab, and their engagement in the subject soared. Why? Because they were in an environment designed to stimulate intellectually curious scientists.

I once visited a private school that hired professional artists and interior decorators to curate classroom spaces with themes that reflected the content area. When I walked into the library, I felt like I was entering a bibliothèque where I wouldn't be surprised to see Josephine Baker and James Baldwin chatting it up or August Wilson sitting in the corner writing his next play. The Italian-language classroom transported me to the streets of Venice. Students could elect to take assessments in designated testing rooms that offered alternatives to fluorescent lights in regular classrooms and limited the number of distracting environmental factors. The message that the school's spaces conveyed to learners was simple: *What you learn and how you learn are equally important. We value you and want to meet your needs.*

Before we ideate on the messages you want your space to convey to learners, let's look at what's **not** working in the typical classroom setup. Read the quote from a fellow educator about the problem with typical classroom setups, and write a short response, as if you were talking to the educator. You might respond with a question, a statement that supports something you agree with, or a relatable example. Here's the quote:

**A fellow educator says:** "Typical classrooms are designed with one-quarter to one-third of the space allocated for the educator and the rest for all of the students. Hierarchy is built into the design; sometimes as an actual stage raised above the rest of the floor. As a student you are expected to sit and listen. You are not in control. You are to passively receive information provided by the educator. You sit facing forward looking at the back of your fellow student heads and at the front wall where content is being shared" (Scott-Webber, 2014).

**Your Response:**

_____

_____

_____

_____

_____

Now, imagine that you shared the quote with your students (in age-appropriate language). How might they respond if you asked them for their opinion?

**Your Students' Responses:**

_____

_____

_____

**What messages would you like your space to convey to learners?** Think of your classroom as a psychologically safe learning environment that fosters the development of healthy academic identities in students. This learning environment is a place where individual and collaborative learning occurs, learner context is embraced, and intellectual curiosity is stimulated.

1. List essential elements needed for your learning environment.

   _____

   _____

   _____

2. How does the knowledge, content, and skills that learners need influence the elements you include?

   _____

   _____

   _____

3. What kind of verbal, visual, and auditory elements might you include?

_____

_____

_____

4. How does your space encourage and support physical action, expression, and communication?

_____

_____

_____

5. What are possible barriers in the space? For whom?

_____

_____

_____

 **Teacher Commentary**

Our school has two branches, both run by different principals. When I was hired as a reading specialist at the upper-grades branch, the administrator didn't tell the principal at the lower-grades branch. Turns out, they were in a dispute over an issue that hadn't been resolved. The office staff didn't know I was coming, so they set me up at the old library which was not being used and overflowing with discarded books and classroom supplies. I felt terrible gathering teachers in that space.

## PURPOSE AND INTENT

The purpose of your classroom is to serve as a gathering space for teaching and learning, which is reflected in your beliefs about how teaching and learning should occur. The design of your space should align with your intention. For example, if your intention is for students to learn from and with one another, then spaces should allow for student–student discourse and the sharing of student work. Rigid rows make student–student discourse more challenging. If your intention is for students to be positioned as scientists, then within your space there should be accessible manipulative tools that help students express their thinking. (Conversely, what message is being conveyed to students when manipulative tools are locked away during teaching and learning, and not within anyone's reach?)

Consider the subject(s) you teach and your beliefs about learning. Assess the extent to which you agree or disagree with the following statements about learning, keeping your content area(s) in mind.

## Activity: Self-Assessment

*Part 1: Assess*

To what extent do you believe the following elements belong in your learning environment?

| | STRONGLY AGREE | SOMEWHAT AGREE | NEITHER AGREE NOR DISAGREE | SOMEWHAT DISAGREE | STRONGLY DISAGREE |
|---|---|---|---|---|---|
| Space to display student thinking and completed student work | | | | | |
| Various types of manipulative tools for students to use | | | | | |
| Multiple areas designated for individual or partner work | | | | | |
| Designated reading or focused study area | | | | | |
| Listening support, such as headphones or speakers | | | | | |
| Library or text-based resources readily available to students | | | | | |

| | STRONGLY AGREE | SOMEWHAT AGREE | NEITHER AGREE NOR DISAGREE | SOMEWHAT DISAGREE | STRONGLY DISAGREE |
|---|---|---|---|---|---|
| Flexible seating arrangement that encourages student–student discourse | | | | | |

*Part 2: Reflect*

1. Review your ratings for each element and consider your learning environment. What is one thing you'd like to enhance? Why?

   _____

   _____

   _____

2. What do students need to feel autonomous in your learning environment?

   _____

   _____

   _____

3. What do students need to feel physically safe in your environment? Psychologically safe?

   _____

   _____

   _____

4. Is there anything hindering you from making changes to your learning environment? What? Explain.

   _____

   _____

   _____

5. What do you have control over changing in your students' learning environment?

_____

_____

_____

**Teacher Commentary**

I like this approach to assessing my students' learning environment because even though I might have physical restrictions in my classroom's physical space, I can start to see beyond these limitations.

**Let's articulate your desired purpose and the intent of your learning environment.** Read the guiding principles for high-quality and effective teaching and learning, some of which are subject-specific. Capture the words, phrases, or sentences that stand out for you because they either align with your beliefs or challenge your thinking. This exercise will help you clarify your beliefs about what you think teaching and learning should be so that you can design your classroom to align with your beliefs.

## Activity: Teaching and Learning Beliefs — Words, Phrases, Relationship to Spaces

*Part 1*

Read the ten guiding principles and record one key word, one phrase, and how each principle relates to spaces.

| | KEY WORD | PHRASE | RELATIONSHIP TO SPACES |
|---|---|---|---|
| 1. Mathematics teaching and learning is most effective when it is centered on student thinking and promotes an asset-based approach to guide instructional decisions. | | | |
| 2. Mathematics teaching and learning is designed to emphasize students' ways of thinking, habits of thinking, and ways of doing mathematics. | | | |

| | KEY WORD | PHRASE | RELATIONSHIP TO SPACES |
|---|---|---|---|
| 3. To develop mathematically, students benefit from having experiences that attend to conceptual understanding, procedural skill and fluency, and application to real-world contexts. | | | |
| 4. Effective math instruction takes into account that all students learn mathematics differently. | | | |
| 5. Literacy involves a multimodal set of skills including reading, writing, speaking, and listening; all modes must be addressed to have a positive impact on students. | | | |
| 6. Literacy undergirds content in every discipline and influences the degree to which students are able to interact with content. | | | |
| 7. Bilingualism is an asset rather than a deficit, and becoming literate in English as a first language and becoming literate in English as a second+ language (e.g., Spanish) are complex, nuanced, and equally deserving of our time, attention, and resources. | | | |
| 8. Effective instruction provides students the unique support they need to become literate in English while honoring their home language. | | | |
| 9. Science teaching, learning, and assessment is centered on meaningful and relevant phenomena, including justice-centered phenomena, that enhance equity by broadening student participation through improved engagement. | | | |
| 10. Assessment is an intrinsic and authentic part of teaching and learning. | | | |

1.  What are some things that pop out for you in the principles?

    _____

    _____

    _____

2.  How might you categorize or sort your choices of key words, phrases, and sentences?

    _____

    _____

    _____

3.  What are some relationships between the words, phrases, and sentences?

    _____

    _____

    _____

4.  What are connections you are making between the guiding principles and your own instruction?

    _____

    _____

    _____

Now, let's articulate a vision for your learning environment. You are the designer of your classroom, which is utilized by a group of diverse students with unique learning needs. You set the stage and tone for learning. You have the opportunity to co-create the learning environment with your students. "When learners believe they have control over their learning environment, they are more likely to take on challenges and persist with difficult tasks, compared with those who perceive that they have little control" (National Research Council, 2018). Your learning environment should appeal to the needs of your learners, and it should function as a space that stimulates a desire to learn. Here are suggestions from eighth graders on how to make their environment into a space where they enjoy teaching and learning:

- Working together in groups more often
- Bigger space to move around

- A temperature that's not too hot or too cold
- Make it clean, much cleaner than you think it is
- Music calms me and helps me work better
- Lots of color
- More comfortable chairs
- Lamps around the room and the ceiling lights off
- More motivational posters
- Outside and inside learning because sitting in the classroom gets boring
- Not having everything on the computers
- Let us decorate the classroom
- Ask us how we think the class should be, not how you think it should be

> *"When we embrace that diversity of experience among our students and recognize that what works for some may not work for others, doors open: We can plan multiple routes for engagement, representation, and expression, which enables more students to succeed." (Ralph, 2021)*

Below are recommendations on the essential spaces to include in a learning environment:

1. Entry zone
2. Work zone
3. Storage system zones
4. Display zones and mini-museums
5. Living things zone
6. Research area and library zone
7. Soft zone
8. Graphic arts
9. Teacher zone
10. Technology zone (Taylor et al., 2011)

## Visualization Exercise

1. Picture your students. Imagine their faces, hear them speaking, and see them moving around. See your students learning, and envision yourself teaching. Now, imagine the space where all of this is taking place. Describe the space. What does it look like? Feel like? Smell like? Sound like? Be as descriptive as possible. Allow yourself to step aside from limitations or restrictions and dwell in possibilities.

   _____

   _____

   _____

2. What might your students say about the learning environment that you visualized and described in #1?

   _____

   _____

   _____

3. Now, list the actual restrictions that you face in your learning environment.

   _____

   _____

   _____

4. Revisit your visualization and identify things that you can put in place with your current restrictions.

   _____

   _____

   _____

# CHAPTER 8

......................................

# SYSTEMS (AND HOW TO THRIVE WITHIN THEM)

*These are the stories of what a student's patience can endure and what a teacher's resolution can achieve.*

**SYSTEMS**

The entry point of systems begs the question, *which systems?* The greater issue of systemic racism? Political systems of legislation and culture wars? Systemic changes in public education? The effective schools movement and systems of factory-model education? The school-to-prison pipeline and racial politics? Redlining and school rezoning? The overprescribing of medications to calm students? The system of behavior referrals? The legal system that takes away your right to say certain words in the classroom?

There are many systems of inequity at play in K–12 education, and they all take a toll on educators at some point during their career. Improving the K–12 education system is a gargantuan undertaking, particularly when so many things at work within the system feel out of a teacher's locus of control. While other books about equity in education tend to focus on systemic racism, this book focuses on the inside-out work that will help you become an equity-empowered

.......................................................................

Image source: NWEA, 2023. Used with permission.

educator. Doing the inner work of equity helps you avoid the trap of **structural equity** — redesigning systems and structures without investing in the deeper personal, interpersonal, and cultural shifts (Safir & Dugan, 2021, p. 33).

I worked in a large, urban school district as a middle-grades math teacher and instructional coach. I used to jokingly say that because of those roles, I could do *anything*. Teachers can attest to the fact that one's personal growth and professional development burgeon when you work day to day with students in the classroom. You develop an unapologetic passion for making a difference in students' lives and a thick skin to shelter you from the pains of working within a (flawed, perfectly designed to be inequitable, or broken) system. I, like most educators, could tell you so many stories about working in education that would touch your pain points and make the amen corner shout.

I started feeling pessimistic, disappointed, and exhausted around my seventh year as an educator. Teacher burnout was real. But no matter how frustrated I became, I always held the enthusiasm of a beginning teacher deep in the recesses of my heart. To remind me of this, my sister bought me a pair of rose-colored sunglasses, a presage of restored hope and a reminder of the vision I held when I became a teacher. I looked through those glasses and shifted my perspective. This chapter isn't about fixing or changing the system; it's about hope.

In this chapter, I'll share the perspectives and advice from fellow educators. I wanted to hear from people who have witnessed and experienced inequities firsthand and gain insight into what they've learned about working through inequities. I hope that their wisdom will energize you so that you can thrive in a system that can sometimes feel draining.

Reflect on the six entry points as you read each story, being mindful of the greater system at play within the story. *What ideas stand out to you in each story? What is the silver lining in the story? What is to be celebrated from the story? How might others tell this story?*

Here are their stories:

- **Cry Loud, Spare Not** — It is our responsibility to be the voice for children when we witness inequities. We must shine a light on inequities and injustices. Even the dimmest light shines bright in a room full of darkness.

- **Working Together We Can Achieve More** — Building safe, collaborative relationships with families can show students that they have multiple adult role models at school, at home, and in their community who work together to support their learning and growth.

- **All Kids Deserve an Opportunity to Succeed** — We teach students, not curriculum. And if we teach students, we shouldn't do the same thing year after year because our students are not the same year after year.

- **Use Assessments to Empower, Not Disempower** — Do not use assessment processes, tools, or results in ways that disempower learners or educators and contributes to or perpetuates educational disparity, toxic stress, and trauma.

- **Keep Going! Keep Growing!** — Move away from a mindset of student compliance and belief that kids must perform for us. This mindset takes us away from developing critical thinkers in kids.

- **When You Know Better, You Do Better** — Teachers can use their experiences as students to empower themselves as educators.

## CRY LOUD, SPARE NOT

Working in public education can take a toll on your emotional, mental, and physical health. It happened to me. Thriving in the industry while keeping your fire ablaze requires inner contentment, compassion for students, and a belief that you are making a difference. My educator friend that you are about to hear from is thriving.

I met my educator friend during her first year of teaching. Even then, her passion for education was strong, and her inner glow was bright. Twenty years and many leadership roles later, she still smiles when she talks about her work. I wanted to know how she maintained her passion after all these years and how she managed to thrive in a school system fraught with inequities.

Her twenty years as an educator include being a middle school math teacher, instructional coach, assistant principal, principal, and leader in several positions at the district office. I admire my friend's relentless efforts to ensure all children have a fair and just chance in school. I trust that her words will inspire you to continue doing equity work for our young people.

I started teaching with a strong passion and burning desire to do the right thing. My first role was at a predominantly Black school in the community where I lived. During the first month of school, my students told me that I was too nice, and I needed to teach kindergarten. I asked them, "Don't you deserve to have someone be nice to you?" I didn't get a response, but they were listening. The next day everyone showed up ready to learn, and that was the first day we actually had school.

My seventh-grade classroom had students ranging from ages 12 to 16. They could see the city skyline from our neighborhood but had never visited downtown. I wanted to take my students

(Continued)

on field trips to see some of our country's best museums that were located right in our city, but I was told that they were too unruly to go out in public. I remember that my prep periods were often canceled because we couldn't get sub coverage. Substitute teachers refused to work at our school because we had such a bad reputation.

I learned that the culture of that school was one of compliance and control. In hindsight, I realize that the interview for that job was a forewarning of the inequities I would experience. About 25 percent of the interview questions were about my skillset, and the other 75 percent were about my ability to keep order in the classroom. One thing is certain, we have a long way to go in the nation as it relates to the public education for Black children.

Over the past couple of decades, I have noticed a drastic difference in how Black children and non-Black children are treated in schools. I've noticed that every student is seen unless they are a Black student. This is an inequity that teachers need to talk about.

The first thing we need to do is honor Black students as humans. You can't work effectively and successfully with children unless you see them as children. You don't even have to see them as "your" kids; just recognize that they are children. Many educators don't see Black children as children — they see them as mini-adults that should know better. The expectation put on Black children is they aren't children. We all know that children are just learning how to be — how to express themselves, how to make sense of the world, how to learn. Yet we expect Black children to not have big feelings, like being angry or ecstatic, and if they do have normal, human feelings they should automatically know how to express them.

I'll never forget the time a teacher passed a student in the hallway. The student, who the teacher didn't know, was visibly distraught, shaken up, and angrily pacing. The teacher interjected by trying to correct the student's behavior — walk straight, calm down, look at me when I talk to you. The teacher's tone probably felt condescending and antagonizing to the student. As a result, the student cursed at the teacher. The teacher said she didn't feel safe, and she fought to get the boy expelled from school!

What that teacher didn't know was that the student was experiencing hard times — raising himself, separated from his siblings, and without any assistance or supports from the state's child welfare system. That student never made any threats to anyone; he was simply angry and needed space to express himself. This lack of compassion from the teacher — her lack of concern or desire to help the student first rather than punish him says so much more about the teacher and the stereotypes and beliefs she held to be true. These harmful beliefs about our children limit our ability to truly do right by them and help them learn and grow.

Black children should not be held to different expectations than non-Black kids. Why is it acceptable for a white student to act out while we deem it a tantrum but if a Black student behaves in the same way they are considered a danger? I encourage teachers to take time to reflect on what it means to be a child.

> *Define child. What does that mean to you? Literally, what does it mean to be a child? What's the experience like? Now, acknowledge that you have a classroom full of children. What are your expectations of them? How do you respond to a child when they are upset and start throwing things in the classroom? Is your natural inclination to think of them as a violent criminal and to feel that your life is in danger? Or are you aware that there is a child who is upset and doesn't know how to articulate their feelings? If your own child exhibited the same behavior, would you call the police on them? Why not?*

All children deserve the chance to succeed. The hard truth is that the system isn't designed for everyone to win; someone has to lose. So as you're fighting for the greater good, recognize that some children will be left behind, but we can still help them grow. I know that is very hard to accept, and it can make you feel sad. I learned that you can't help everyone, but we can help to make every student's learning experience better. It's hard work but we have to do it for all kids:

- The kids who won't have support at home
- The children who lack intrinsic motivation
- The learners who are victims of circumstance
- The students whose gifts we don't tap into
- The students that we overlook

Despite all of the inequities I've witnessed over the years I still love what I do. That's because I love the kids. I see myself in the kids — someone who is curious about the world and wants to learn and grow — and that's what keeps me going. But I know it's very hard for teachers right now. Teaching is so much more than teaching. I've noticed a lot more impatience with children postpandemic.

The reality is that some educators are tired of working with children. It seems that educators' intolerance is much higher and the expectations for students to perform make educators want to resort directly to consequences rather than putting in supports for students or making interventions. Our classroom environments have become more punitive. I've seen educators use district and school policy against students, saying things like "the school community is not safe" or "this child is upsetting the emotional and academic well-being of others." This aggressive language creates a toxic culture. And it's hard to work in that type of environment. My advice to teachers is to guard your heart.

(Continued)

*(Continued)*

I cry aloud and spare not when it comes to Black children. We need to do that for all children. It is our responsibility to be the voice for children when we witness inequities. We must shine a light on inequities and injustices. Even the dimmest light shines bright in a room full of darkness. I know that equity work is hard. Just remember to do your best. Do the best you can with what you have for the students under your care. You are making a difference!

## WORKING TOGETHER, WE CAN ACHIEVE MORE

I believe that most parents and families want to have a role in their child's education. Parent-teacher conferences are a great way to engage in the child's teaching and learning experience, but life can get in the way. It can be difficult to find a time that works for parents and families to attend the conferences. Language barriers might prevent families from attending. Sometimes parents have anxiety or apprehension about meeting with their child's teacher, especially if they didn't have good experiences as a student.

I asked a seasoned educator to reflect on her experience teaching and how knowing more about learner and family/caregiver context could inform ways to invite students and their families/caregivers into a nurturing, collaborative learning space. Her various roles as an educator have given her firsthand experience with the power of collaboration between teachers, leaders, parents, and community members. Here is her story:

A school I worked with as part of a statewide curriculum and technology grant initiative struggled to not only increase attendance at parent–teacher conferences but to increase attendance at family events that were part of the grant. In the second year of the grant, we put forth a concerted effort to increase family engagement — and not simply for the project but because we knew the impact of good relationships between school and home.

The entire staff began the effort to increase attendance at conferences and grant events by meeting families where they were. Surveys gathered information to support the effort. Schedules were created to accommodate parents/caregivers who worked during the day so they could have a time that met their availability. If transportation was an obstacle, then transportation was either provided or teachers scheduled meetings at students' homes or shelters if that was the case — whether that was with a parent, grandparent, or other relative. For some families, those choices were not seen as a safe space, so alternatives were suggested and asked for. For some families, that meant the public library, local church, snack bar at Walmart, etc.

We wanted to build safe, collaborative relationships between students and families. Teachers learned that for some parents, school was a traumatic experience, and they did not want to relive that and/or hear that their students were having the same experiences. For others, their work simply did not allow for the typical times that conferences and other events were scheduled, and they did not feel empowered to advocate and ask for optional times. And for some families, as much as they wanted to be involved and engaged, the last thing they wanted was for others to be in their homes, so other location options removed that barrier. Our communication with families emphasized collaboration and working together to meet the needs of students in the spirit of creating a partnership with open communication.

What resulted over time was 100 percent attendance rate for conferences and other grant events! But more importantly, we increased communication and collaboration between school and home. Students saw that they had multiple adult role models at school, at home, and in their community who they knew were working together to support their learning and growth. What a great impact that grant helped us make!

## ALL KIDS DESERVE AN OPPORTUNITY TO SUCCEED

There were times when I taught middle school math without enough textbooks for all my students. Sometimes I felt that the curriculum was very limiting, not allowing enough opportunities for students to explore different ways of thinking about math and applying math to other contexts outside the classroom. Lack of proper materials put me and my students at a disadvantage. My students had already developed disdain for mathematics, thinking it was boring, hard, and unnecessary. Their respect for the subject dwindled when we didn't have adequate textbooks or supplies. It was very hard to survive, let alone thrive, in such a learning environment.

Whenever I saw this one particular educator in action — teaching math to kids or adults — she made the content come alive with or without textbooks and materials. I sat down with her to learn more about how we can help students thrive in mathematics.

This dynamic educator has been a math teacher, instructional coach, and assistant principal in K–12 in a large, urban school district. She believes that mathematics shouldn't be a gatekeeper subject that excludes learners and educators because it is presented as "special," "elite," or only accessible for mastery by a select few. This equity-empowered educator believes that math is for everyone.

The insights from our interview have been edited for clarity.

**Fenesha Hubbard:** Some people don't believe that equity is a worthwhile topic, or they fail to see how it relates to their teaching or learning for their students. What do you think about that?

**Math Educator:** I don't know that people who are in most dire need of equity work understand how inequitable things really are right now because they cannot fathom how good those who have it, have it. They don't understand what's possible because they haven't had access to all possibilities. Consider this analogy where you offer two people a gift of anything they want. The first person asks for something that costs $50, and the other person asks for something that costs $2,000. The first person limited their cost option because they couldn't ever imagine that there is more money available. People who are so accustomed to having very little are used to making do with very little. Therefore, they have limited their expectations.

**Fenesha:** You've worked in a large, urban school district. What advice do you have for educators whose hands feel tied by such a system?

**Math Educator:** There are a lot of educators that practice benchmark grading or competency-based grading standards, because of district mandates. They set the standards to be at the middle of the bell curve or the norm. Or educators feel that if students reach academic proficiency, then they've met the standard. And if academic proficiency is the standard the educators set for all students, then it's not high enough. Math equity means everybody getting what they need to be on equal footing. The standards are the bare minimum. Educators need to consider what students are required to know in relation to the standards and what they need to know to apply math in other contexts. Equity doesn't just mean meeting the standard so that we show gains, that we show academic proficiency, or that we receive funding. Equity means giving students what they need to fully participate in society. In order to be equitable, we need to adjust the benchmark and reconsider the goal. The goal shouldn't be just to pass this test because there are a lot of students who might have passed the test but don't understand how to apply the concepts outside of the context of the math classroom.

**Fenesha:** How can we shift our assessment practices to be more equitable?

**Math Educator:** Look at the inequities — aiming for the bubble kids in the middle so that we can get the scores we need (for the district or the state) is inequitable. Instead, we should work to meet the needs of students who have the greatest needs and even the students who exceed the standards. Every learner deserves to have an opportunity to grow. If we have low standards for students who are at the top, what happens when they go to the next grade? Their academic identity is challenged because up until that point they believed they were excelling, but educators were measuring their excellence against a low target, so now they are no longer excelling.

**Fenesha:** What about teachers' academic identities?

**Math Educator:** Teachers must always strengthen their academic identity. There's a different way to approach teaching altogether where we move beyond showing students how to do things. By finding instructional strategies that turn learners' brains on and engage them in teaching and learning, you're expanding your academic identity as a teacher. Remember that equity means giving every single learner what they need to be on equal footing. It also means giving yourself as an educator the tools to help students grow.

**Fenesha:** What's one practical thing teachers can do right now?

**Math Educator:** Find out what students need. The only way to find out what students need is to find out what they know, and we do that through dialogue and inquiry. We consider the opportunities we are giving our students to learn about math, talk about math, and share their thinking. Teachers need to reframe how they think about their role as a teacher. Good math teaching is not about your ability to lecture and have students regurgitate facts and procedures.

**Fenesha:** Is there anything we're not talking about in the equity conversation?

**Math Educator:** Educators need to also consider how they talk about student performance and how they define success. What messages are we sending to learners about what it means to be successful? What are the behaviors of a successful student in math class? Are the same students always the exemplars for success? If so, there is an inequity somewhere that needs to be examined and corrected. Equity in math requires that we create opportunities to succeed for all students. We create spaces and situations where students can explore their thinking, reflect on their work, and get to the point where they can say that they are proud of their work. Equity in the classroom means giving students a voice to share what they know and what they are contemplating. It means ensuring that they have a sense of belonging and feel safe to question their thinking and the thinking of their peers.

**Fenesha:** What final words do you have for our fellow educators?

**Math Educator:** All kids deserve an opportunity to succeed. We teach students, not curriculum. And if we teach students, we shouldn't do the same thing year after year because our students are not the same year after year.

 **Teacher Commentary**

▶ I hope that this resonates strongly with teachers. If a student has decided that they are "good/bad at math," are "not a reader," or are "smart/not smart," then they will live up to their belief about themselves — good or bad. Turning that belief around for students who have given up is key to helping students be successful.

(Continued)

*(Continued)*

> ▶ I had a student who was born and raised in Germany. He had learned a different process to solve multidigit multiplication problems. He struggled to accurately multiply in the way our fifth-grade textbook described. But when I gave him an opportunity to demonstrate his method to the class, several other students started using that process because it made more sense to them.

## USE ASSESSMENTS TO EMPOWER, NOT DISEMPOWER

This is my story. In my first year of teaching, I learned how powerful and dangerous assessments and data can be when they are used solely to manage learning rather than empower learners. Two instances stand out in my mind. The first was when Keith, a nine-year-old who loved to volunteer in my classroom, broke down crying one day after school. "Ms. Hubbard, I just can't take it anymore. I'm tired of all these tests." Keith's only job was to be a lover of learning and a kid. If he carried that much stress from testing at his age, a massive overhaul of how we do assessments was needed. The second time it was an incident that taught me that if we don't use assessments and data with an equity focus, we risk weaponizing it against our students.

It was a typical fall day in my math class and students' body language let me know they were so engaged in the learning that they forgot to stay seated. I saw young people helping their peers think through problems. Others were working together to solve math tasks. I moved among my students, spending about ten minutes with each group. But on this one seemingly normal day, the environment I created that was full of empowered learners shifted.

The intercom switched on and someone blared, "Ms. Hubbard, you need to stop what you're doing and bring your class to the auditorium to receive their test results." The eighth graders belted out a chorus of "awwwww dang!" and my student Aisha asked, "Ms. Hubbard, why do they treat us like this? Always interrupting!" Neither my students nor I wanted to be taken out of an engaging classroom lesson to experience what was likely to be more unwarranted deprecation from school leaders — a common thing whenever we talked about student test scores.

The eighth graders' test scores would determine their academic pathways for the next four years. Some would attend a traditional public high school, others would test into magnet schools, and a few would be granted admission to a selective school — often among the highest performing. Their scores would also judge whether I was an effective teacher. This was weaponization of data at its worst and misunderstanding of assessment at its best.

Neither my students nor I had insight into how the results were going to be presented, addressed, or used. I gathered my class and tried to prepare them for this data-revealing experience. Perhaps each student would be handed a sheet of paper with their numbers in red ink. Maybe they'd meet with the school counselor. Possibly we'd be seated for an uplifting and inspirational speech, and the test scores would be our exit ticket from the auditorium. My students and I walked into the unknown with anxiety and trepidation.

Our principal handed out the scores, and one by one, I saw my students receiving them as personal judgments. Shoulders slumped, heads began to hang, and weeping ensued. I felt powerless because our school administrators were giving full permission for this weaponization of data. **Weaponization of data** is the use of scores to punish students and teachers, which can further set back already disadvantaged groups of people. More specifically, weaponization of data is

> [t]he use of assessment processes, tools, or results in ways that disempower learners or educators and contributes to or perpetuates educational disparity, toxic stress, and trauma. (Erin Beard, M.Ed, D.Ed)

Weaponization of data is hardly ever (hopefully, probably never) intentional. I used assessments and data to empower my students. The school utilized processes that created barriers "between assessments that drive student learning and assessments that measure school performance" (Minnich, 2020). The test my students took was designed to inform instruction. The student data from the test was supposed to help me determine which practices to employ to teach students at their individual levels of readiness. However, we used an interim test for summative purposes. We made assessment a punitive process that harmed, rather than helped, our students. Assessment was something we did to students, and they felt used.

Assessment and data are valuable tools that we need to inform teaching and learning. However, despite decades of research, the use of assessments and data continue to be problematic. Rather than letting assessment serve as a process that promotes student agency and success, it serves as something we do to students. The widely believed myth is that assessment is a test or quiz. If an educator believes this to be true, then they will likely do tasks that result in a score or design assessments that don't actually serve the intended purpose (i.e., a dominant cultural perspective that assesses for privilege or language, rather than content). Again, there is nothing inherently wrong with assigning a task to measure performance, but what would be possible if we expanded our definition of assessment and data from a single test or event to an embedded process in teaching and learning?

I encourage educators to challenge systems that use assessment in punitive ways. Sometimes we have to unlearn what we've been taught about assessment and data, and here are a few questions to help you unpack what you have learned:

1. Think back to when you started teaching. How did you learn what assessments were and how they were to be used? What messages were you given about assessments?

2. Do you tend to think of assessment as an *event* or a process? Why?

3. Are there disparities between how your assessments are intended to be used and how your assessment processes are actually experienced?

## KEEP GOING! KEEP GROWING!

The following story is from an experienced classroom teacher and administrator whom I've worked with in education. Since becoming an educator, she has sought to understand how K–12 education works to help students succeed, and has relentlessly aimed to make teaching and learning better for students. Her story was edited for clarity.

My first year of teaching was in a predominantly Black school in a city on the opposite side of the country from where I'd lived. I assumed that because I was a teacher who looked like my students (I'm Black) and cared about them, that we would easily understand each other. After a few weeks of teaching, I quickly learned that it takes a lot more than looking like your students to build relationships with them.

My students were several years behind academically. Some were too old to be in eighth grade, having been held back in previous grades. I had students that were passed on to the next grade although they were not academically ready. So I thought that I needed to take control of the classroom because that's what I saw successful teachers do when I was a student. Most of my teachers did a lot of lecturing, and I thought that worked.

There was a student I taught for two years in a row, back-to-back grades. Let's call him Jamond, for the sake of the story. Jamond seemed to be suffering from depression and some anxiety. I met with his mother, and we both tried to problem-solve ways to support him. It was hard to build a relationship with Jamond the first year. I often told him "I'm never going to give up on you." He was very closed off emotionally, and there were days when he'd sit in the class and not do any work. Sometimes, it was just that his basic needs weren't met, so anything related to classwork was not priority for him. I always made sure to ask Jamond what he needed, and I offered suggestions for things that might help, like taking a short break or doing a different activity. I think I was a good teacher. I tried my best. I had high expectations for kids. I just needed to strengthen my relationships with students, and especially Jamond.

During that second year, I changed the way I approached the student–teacher relationship. I decided that the relationship goes both ways: I learn from them, and they learn from me. I was better able to admit when I was wrong, and I practiced being honest with students. Instead of acting as the "authoritarian sage on stage," I shifted to being the facilitator of learning.

I tried to find as many different ways that I could to show Jamond that he was capable of success and that I was not going to give up on trying to help him realize that. If I saw that he was working on something correctly, I'd discreetly tell him that his answer was correct and that I was going to call on him to share his thinking and his answer with the class. One day he jokingly said, "Forget this, I'm going to the other class!" I nonchalantly said, "Oh, okay. Go ahead." So Jamond replied, "But you said you weren't going to ever give up on me." I smiled and told him that I was joking, just as he was. All that time I didn't know he'd really taken my words to heart.

Jamond truly believed that I was never going to give up on him — not just because of my words, but because my words were backed up by my actions. Even when he pushed back, I stayed consistent. He saw me attempting to "see" him. And that was when Jamond began to really show up and engage as a student. Guess what? So did the other students in my class! I never gave up on my students, and I feel like that's what teachers are supposed to do. Never giving up didn't mean continuing the same thing over and over; it meant finding new ways to connect and engage — and asking students what they need.

My students had been through eight years of feeling unsuccessful, feeling like teachers didn't care about them, and having high teacher turnaround in a single school year. They didn't trust me at first — rightfully so. In the beginning, I was a teacher with very high expectations, and I was no-nonsense. I didn't give a lot of room for human mistakes, and that caused me to bump heads with my students a lot. I had a lot of compassion for my students in that first year, but I didn't have strong connections with them until the second year.

I got to the point where my students challenged me but in a good way. I think one of the greatest indicators of respect is when a student can tell me that they think I'm wrong and justify

(Continued)

their reason or raise their hand to clarify something I said. I love when students are curious about how their peers think and are open to other perspectives. This shows that students feel they have agency. Students need to know that their perspective matters, and they need to feel affirmed by us — their teachers. Working to get students engaged in teaching and learning this way is how you make a difference.

A lot of the teaching that I've seen is driven by student compliance: Are they doing what I tell them to do? I think that a lot of teachers have the mindset that kids must perform for us, and academic performance becomes compliance based. This mindset takes us away from developing critical thinkers in kids.

There was a seventh-grade teacher, a white woman, who often reported that her students made her cry. In her opinion, the students wouldn't behave or were too loud. She didn't feel that she could "control" her class. Our eighth-grade team of teachers were all Black women. The admin thought that our eighth-grade team wouldn't have the same issues with certain students — and we didn't. But rather than help the seventh-grade teacher learn how to establish and build better relationships with students and find ways to connect with them, the students were just passed along. We penalized the students, which happens far too often, instead of helping that teacher improve her practice and shift her mindset.

I can understand how challenging it is because at times it can be frustrating to figure out what to do, and to do that with all of your students is a lot. But it's what makes a difference in the classroom. Every child matters.

Suppose the data says 45 percent of Black males in a certain city don't graduate college. That does not mean that you only teach the half of the kids in the class or half of the Black males in the class. Yes, the data is discouraging, and the work of teaching can feel like a struggle that keeps you up at night. Still, your responsibility is to show up every day and teach to 100 percent of the Black males and all students in your classroom. A lot of us feel like no matter how hard we try to help each and every student, it is still not going to be enough because at the end of the day, the statistics show that the student is going to be in the same or worse situation. Yes, there are many outliers, but not enough to feel like you're making a difference. Your goal is to try to change that 45 percent graduation rate to 47 percent and then to 49 percent. Small movements are the movements that add up to big movements.

We have to believe and trust that the work we do makes a difference. I really think mindsets are important. I've always been passionate about making sure that I'm a continuously developing educator — always becoming a better version of myself for students, which will result in a better education for students. I've come a long way, and I know other educators will also!

## WHEN YOU KNOW BETTER, YOU DO BETTER

Here are some poignant examples of how K–12 educators had their academic identity damaged by teachers when they were students. After that are reflections from those same educators in their role as teachers. As you read the examples, notice how many are relatable to you or educators that you know and how people chose to do better and be better teachers based on the inequities they experienced as students.

Here's how my academic identity got damaged as a student:

- "I remember being called dumb by my ninth-grade teacher. When I got to my first high school, I was placed on the 'dumb' side of the classroom. The teacher administered a 10-point quiz, and if you got below 8.5 out of 10 on the quiz, you were placed on the dumb side of the classroom. This was a Catholic all-girls school, so no one, except my mom, was upset by that term."

- "My teacher in fifth grade accused me of cheating to get the right answer, when in fact I was just doing it the way my dad taught me at home, and he's a math teacher!"

- "My twelfth-grade English teacher thought I had plagiarized my senior paper. She said that she didn't think I could write that well. In reality, I didn't get excited about assignments in her class until the senior paper, where I could write passionately about the topic of my choice."

- "We had a rural school district that categorized most Hispanic students in the Title III / LET / ELL program. The students spoke English as well as native English speakers but felt dumb or labeled as 'less than' because they were wrongfully placed. The students were mostly second or third generation in the United States, but the district received funding for documenting the students. Once people realized how inequitable this was, the district was required to 'exit' the majority of their students from the ELL program."

- "I was transferred into Honors English in the middle of the semester, and it was my first day. I was excited to participate in an honors classroom! One day, I answered a question aloud and mistakenly repeated a racial slur that was used in the text we were reading. It was the first time I'd ever heard the term. The teacher scolded me in front of the class. I would've appreciated the teacher explaining why the word was inappropriate, instead of publicly scolding me. That humiliating experience ruined the way I participated in class from that moment forward. I didn't want to take chances nor raise my hand anymore for fear of being scolded again."

(Continued)

*(Continued)*

- "In high school, I remember shying away from science courses. I lacked confidence in understanding the content and dropped class. Now I know that it wasn't that I couldn't learn the content, rather it was that the teacher lacked the tools to differentiate the content for me as a contextual learner. I wish I had someone nudge me to step up and take that academic risk."

- "I loved the sciences in high school. I had hopes of studying biology in college and becoming a physical therapist. In tenth grade, I received the outstanding biology student award. But in eleventh grade, my chemistry teacher gave me the 'lead test tube award' in front of everyone for being the worse chemistry student of all his classes. I was devastated and from that point on, I shied away from anything 'scientific.'"

- "I grew up in foster care. I'm Jewish and lived in the poorer parts of town. It was tenth grade when I just found a home after being homeless, and I returned to school late in the term. I remember a teacher told me that I lacked the focus and drive to make anything of myself and that I should definitely not be on the college track."

- "My second-grade teacher told us she didn't like students or teaching. Then, she made me do all of the work assigned to my classmate who broke his arm. I'm still confused by her teaching style to this day."

Here's how I used inequities I experienced to empower me as a teacher:

- "When I first started teaching, I was very confrontational when I saw actions/words that were harmful to kids, but I quickly learned that didn't change people's behaviors. Only through trust, rapport, and building bridges was I able to help teachers question their own practices and biases to create supportive and equity-focused classrooms. I quickly found out who I could impact and which teachers were too far gone, but all in all, seeking to understand who teachers want to be and who they are is a great starting point to helping academic identities become equity-focused. I've seen multiple instances where teachers put their special education students at a back table by themselves to do 'folder work' which was never grade level, often too easy, and sometimes just consisted of coloring pages instead of involving them with the grade-level instruction with the rest of the class. I've even seen administrators condone this behavior because 'they're too low to get anything anyways' or 'they can't do the work anyways.' By being seated at the back, isolated, and given different work, they were being told that they weren't smart enough to be with the class or be involved with the classroom community. They were being told they would never be smart enough to join the rest of the class. They were being ostracized. They were being labeled as 'different.' This was first modeled by the teacher and then mimicked by the other students in the class, and it easily — and sadly — became a part of their identity."

- "I used to have a traditional view that hard work and being part of the system would get you through this game of school. As I've gotten to learn more about equity, my perspective of equity has drastically changed. It's all intertwined with one another and the system can be disrupted at any point to benefit our students. Thinking through my academic identity has definitely helped me understand my learning journey more clearly. Unfortunately, I thought through it after my teaching career. I can still use my new experiences and understanding of my academic journey to help other current educators consider theirs."

- "I knew that as a teacher I was in a position of power that could have a majorly positive or majorly negative impact on my students. I tried to act in a way that would be positive. But thinking back, if I had been familiar with the concept of an 'academic identity,' I might have been more purposeful about how I shaped that positive impact. I had students who were identified with 'learning disabilities,' and while they were successful, I wish now that I had done more to make sure that they didn't feel like they were labeled by their diagnosis. Or that I had better acknowledge how their hard work had led them to be successful and how that was an advantage that they had over some of their peers for whom things came easily. We know that white, dominant culture means that white students have a lot of advantages when it comes to school and are poised to have better academic identities than students of color. As a teacher, part of my job is to make sure that I cultivate a positive academic identity for all of my students."

- "Poking at identity can be hard work and stir up strong feelings, including rage. When I questioned colleagues' use of the words 'mama's boy' or 'sissy' with students or when I asked a colleague to use a student's name instead of a nickname about her heritage, I was called a bully and harassed. For engaging and sustaining this hard work, I recommend surrounding oneself with strong mentors, allies, and advocates."

- "We got our class list a few days before school started during my first year. My mentor teacher showed me his 'helpful tip' of how he checked the addresses listed for each student to look for street names from a particular neighborhood. He said that kids from that neighborhood struggled in school and were behavior problems, so I needed to 'watch out' for them. I had one student on my list from that neighborhood, and she ended up being a bright, thoughtful, caring student. I was thrilled that she proved him wrong."

## WHAT'S YOUR STORY?

The entry points for equity are within our stories, and our stories provide insight into what needs to change in order to create more equitable teaching and learning experiences for students. The more we learn from one another's experiences, the greater the chances for better understanding and collective growth.

I invite you to tell your story. Some of the ways you might begin are to think of . . .

- How you came to be an educator
- What has been working well for you
- When you handled a tough situation well
- When you made a real contribution
- When you felt strongly connected to your students
- How your values come through in your teaching
- When you felt respected and honored as a teacher
- When you tried something new
- What helps you do your very best (Tschannen-Moran & Tschannen-Moran, 2010, p. 67)

What story do you want to tell? After you write your story, share your story with a 180- or 360-partner. Ask them what ideas stand out in your story? Which entry points are in your story? How might they tell your story?

Much of the work in this book involved inner work. Sharing your story is part of the outer work that can help transform systems. May we tell our stories and find within them solutions that can help shape the structures that form our systems.

# CHAPTER 9

## ACTIVATING THE ENTRY POINTS

Our overall goal is to make equity actionable and visible in the practices and outcomes of our work. We're doing that by starting with the entry points for equity and deep empathy. Entry points are the contexts where we have opportunities to act on our equity values. We're using empathy as a

Image source: NWEA, 2023. Used with permission.

tool because by better understanding how we each experienced equity (or inequities), we can get a clearer sense of what practices and outcomes might look like for student success.

Empathy, which differs from sympathy, allows us to be compassionate toward learners and educators. "Sympathy is identifying with another person's experience primarily on an emotional level. We feel the pain of another as our pain and the joy of another as our joy. . . . Empathy requires a conscious treasuring of emotions as the gateway to learning, growth, and change. Although sympathy utilizes some of the same faculties as empathy and can offer clues as to what the other person may be experiencing, it doesn't engage the deeper faculties of consciousness, reflection, and choice required for emotional processing and transformation" (Tschannen-Moran & Tschannen-Moran, 2010, p. 88).

Let's start with an empathy exercise to identify what we expect to see and hear among colleagues as we begin our equity work.

## WINDOWS AND MIRRORS

Lacey Robinson of UnboundEd uses the term *equity architects* when describing teachers who are empowered to enact equity. Equity architects create the context for the learning experiences they deliver and demonstrate that teaching equitably is both a skill and a conscious activity. Equity architects recognize equity in action as the critical lens through which we create and deliver learning. If we see ourselves as equity architects, then we need to start by looking at the blueprints we create in our minds.

Before activating the entry points, you and your team should surface all assumptions and expectations you have about engaging in equity work. **Windows and Mirrors** is a visioning activity that "provides a psychologically safe way for a group to gain insights into their own process and relationship skills. This strategy uses visualization to enable group members to take an outside, or third person, perspective, describing what they might see through a window or reflected in a mirror." This activity will help you better understand how you and your team can work together effectively. (Note: This activity differs from the "Curriculum as Window and Mirror" metaphor by Emily Jane Styles.)

Set aside 15 to 20 minutes to complete this activity, and then an additional 15 minutes to reflect alone, and 30 minutes to discuss with colleagues.

**Step 1: WINDOW** – Imagine that you are viewing your colleagues through a special one-way window as they discuss equity. Describe what you are seeing and hearing.

**Step 2: MIRROR** – Imagine that you are leading a discussion about equity among your colleagues. You can observe your own behavior, which is reflected in mirrored walls. What do you see and hear yourself doing?

| WINDOW | | MIRROR | |
|---|---|---|---|
| Imagine that you are viewing your colleagues through a special one-way window as they discuss equity. Describe what you are seeing and hearing. | | Imagine that you are leading a discussion about equity among your colleagues. You can observe your own behavior, which is reflected in mirrored walls. What do you see and hear yourself doing? | |
| SEE | HEAR | SEE | HEAR |
| | | | |
| | | | |
| | | | |
| | | | |
| | | | |

Windows and Mirrors is an exercise in reflection that can be completed alone but is best done with a group. Here are responses that you might see a group generate when doing this activity together:

| WINDOW | | MIRROR | |
|---|---|---|---|
| Imagine that you are viewing your colleagues through a special one-way window as they discuss equity. Describe what you are seeing and hearing. | | Imagine that you are leading a discussion about equity among your colleagues. You can observe your own behavior, which is reflected in mirrored walls. What do you see and hear yourself doing? | |
| SEE | HEAR | SEE | HEAR |
| A room full of teachers that are very present and not distracted | Lots of "I" statements | I'm scanning the room to notice people's reactions | I'm asking a lot of probing questions |
| Lots of straight faces, few smiles | Silence at first, then people are eager to chime in | I'm taking notes on what's being said and capturing highlights on chart paper for everyone to see | I'm being quiet to allow room for others to contribute to the conversation |

(Continued)

| SEE | HEAR | SEE | HEAR |
|---|---|---|---|
| Guarded behaviors in speech | An inability to connect the discussion to the classroom | Visible frustration because someone feels like this is always a "special topic" | It feels like I'm speaking into a vacuum |
| People not talking but if there are people of color in the room then they are often leading the discussion | Maybe someone accidentally saying something insensitive and hurtful | An overprepared presentation to hide the fact that I'm uncomfortable talking about this topic in school | A lot of verbal and nonverbal affirmation to encourage participation |
| Uncertainty and fear of being vulnerable | Questions asked to hear other perspectives | Being critical of myself | Lots of listening |
| Open posture or crossed arms | Silence | Sharing my own experiences and acknowledging that I'm not an expert | Some judgment in people's responses |
| Teachers writing reflections and taking notes | People grappling with but embracing their discomfort | Teachers sharing examples from their classroom experiences | People owning the fact that we all have biases |

**Windows and Mirrors** is designed to help you and your team "bring outcomes and explicit success criteria to the center of the [equity] conversation" (Lipton & Wellman, 2010, p. 21). The things you listed in the "See" column can be used to pinpoint the assumptions you hold about your colleagues and the role you contribute to the group. The things you listed in the "Hear" column are indicative of group norms and culture. Collectively, the items generated from this activity will help you better understand the relational knowledge, or awareness of the self and other, that everyone brings to the conversation.

I recommend conducting this activity with your group and then identifying any themes, assumptions, and expectations you collectively notice in the responses. Use those responses to establish group working agreements — five to ten statements that indicate how people will participate in conversations around equity, which will allow for healthy dialogue in a psychologically safe space.

You can use the responses in the "See" column to be proactive: If we notice a fear of vulnerability, how might we respond? If everyone is not equally contributing to the conversation, what protocols or norms might we reference to create a safer space for sharing?

Once you've taken time to look into your windows and mirrors, you are ready to examine inequities.

## Teacher Commentary

When I imagine Windows and Mirrors in action, I hear people tiptoeing around topics. I see everyone being very serious. Folxs of color are tired of being called upon to speak as the sole arbitrator of their experiences. White folxs are too nervous to share their actual thoughts out of fear of being labeled a racist. No one is discussing neurodiversity. Antisemitism is not discussed or even considered, along with any discussion on LBTQIA+, or non-Christian identities. In the end, it's a lot of talk and no action. I want us to acknowledge that we are all imperfect in our understanding of and acting on equity. We fail because we are human. We need to recognize that we are different. We're not here to play oppression Olympics. We are here to learn from one another.

## ENTRY POINT EXAMPLES

Equity is a broad topic. I've introduced the entry points for equity as a way to identify specific opportunities for more equitable practice within schools. Think about what you've learned about the entry points for equity in this book. Take a few minutes to reflect on what you understand about the entry points and what you need to explore and learn more about. I encourage you to discuss your responses with a colleague or peer group.

## REFLECTION

*Got it!* – What do you understand about the entry points for equity?

*Need it!* – What do you need to explore and learn more about?

|  | GOT IT! | NEED IT! |
|---|---|---|
| Mindsets |  |  |
| Relationships |  |  |
| Products |  |  |
| Processes |  |  |
| Spaces |  |  |
| Systems |  |  |

Examining inequities is a great way to begin thinking about how you can operationalize equity. Below are examples of inequities, juxtaposed with an equity. Read the inequity, and reflect on whether you've encountered a similar inequity. Then, rate your readiness to enter the equity conversation, indicating whether the example is new to you, familiar but unclear why it's an inequity, makes sense and you see why it's an inequity, or one that you've seen and acted upon.

Remember, wherever you enter the equity conversation is fine, just as long as you enter with an openness to learn, grow, and change. This is a self-reflection, not an evaluation or judgment.

| ENTRY POINT | INEQUITY | EQUITY | SELF-ASSESSMENT |
| --- | --- | --- | --- |
| Mindsets | Some teachers believe that students lack the background knowledge needed to be involved in the goal-setting process. | The administrators and/or coaches work to shift the mindset and help teachers see goal-setting as a practice, supporting all students to set goals and achieve them. | This example is:<br><br>• New to me. I've not seen it in action before.<br><br>• Familiar, but I don't understand why it's an inequity.<br><br>• Making sense and I'm aware of why it's an inequity.<br><br>• One I've seen and I've helped, or witnessed others, guide teachers toward enacting the equity. |
| Relationships | In front of the class, the teacher calls out the students who did not finish their assignments and announces that their grades will be affected. | The teacher talks individually to each student about finishing the required assignment and asks if there is something specific that is hindering them from finishing the work. | This example is:<br><br>• New to me. I've not seen it in action before.<br><br>• Familiar, but I don't understand why it's an inequity.<br><br>• Making sense and I'm aware of why it's an inequity.<br><br>• One I've seen and I've helped, or witnessed others, guide teachers toward enacting the equity. |

| ENTRY POINT | INEQUITY | EQUITY | SELF-ASSESSMENT |
|---|---|---|---|
| Products | Our interim assessments are only available in English and Spanish. For students whose native language is not Spanish or English, the only option is the English tests. The data isn't disaggregated for beginning-level English learners. | We use additional data points (e.g., scores on English-language proficiency tests) to triangulate data and get a more accurate picture of students' needs and progress. | This example is:<br><br>• New to me. I've not seen it in action before.<br><br>• Familiar, but I don't understand why it's an inequity.<br><br>• Making sense and I'm aware of why it's an inequity.<br><br>• One I've seen and I've helped, or witnessed others, guide teachers toward enacting the equity. |
| Spaces | A teacher pulls students out of class and into reading groups that unintentionally create spaces that feel psychologically unsafe. | Using assessment data, the teacher creates instructionally focused guided-reading groups that provide all students access to complex, grade-level text, including scaffolding as needed. | This example is:<br><br>• New to me. I've not seen it in action before.<br><br>• Familiar, but I don't understand why it's an inequity.<br><br>• Making sense and I'm aware of why it's an inequity.<br><br>• One I've seen and I've helped, or witnessed others, guide teachers toward enacting the equity. |
| Processes | A teacher meets only with groups of students who need support because they don't have time to meet with all students. The teacher prioritizes students who are "struggling." | A teacher creates groups based on all needs, including enrichment, and all students are included in groups that the teacher meets with on a weekly basis. | This example is:<br><br>• New to me. I've not seen it in action before.<br><br>• Familiar, but I don't understand why it's an inequity.<br><br>• Making sense and I'm aware of why it's an inequity.<br><br>• One I've seen and I've helped, or witnessed others, guide teachers toward enacting the equity. |

(Continued)

*(Continued)*

| ENTRY POINT | INEQUITY | EQUITY | SELF-ASSESSMENT |
|---|---|---|---|
| Systems | Between the three junior English teachers, late-work processes and policies vary greatly. One teacher accepts late work up to the end of the term with no penalty. Another teacher takes 10 percent off the score each day the work is late. The third teacher doesn't accept late work at all and enters a zero for the grade after the deadline. | The three junior English teachers discuss the potential (and unintentional) inequities that their different grading processes and policies can cause for various students (like those who work or take care of siblings after school). They agree that their common goal is to support learning. They also come to agree that grade reductions don't effectively motivate students to complete work and, therefore, don't support learning. | This example is:<br><br>• New to me. I've not seen it in action before.<br><br>• Familiar, but I don't understand why it's an inequity.<br><br>• Making sense and I'm aware of why it's an inequity.<br><br>• One I've seen and I've helped, or witnessed others, guide teachers toward enacting the equity. |

 **Teacher Commentary**

▶ Entry points are the key to equity. Too many of us teachers approach equity work as just another thing to do or a checklist of things to add to our teaching or curriculum. Without the entry points, we can hide behind preconceived notions and not come to terms with our academic identities, biases, and racist ideologies. Entry points literally provide the entry points for the real work of equity to begin.

▶ I've seen all of these examples of inequities in schools, and I see the equity-based solutions so clearly. The challenge is understanding the context around the relationships with a teacher that are a part of the problem, power dynamics related to school-based roles, and essentially what is going to effect change: a stern conversation or empathy. (Is that too soft when children are at-risk?) Sometimes I get analysis-paralysis with these tough decisions resulting in no action and a lot of guilt. None of this is easy, but it is necessary.

Please note that there could be many more complex and diverse examples. Also, keep in mind that there are situational overlaps of inequities and equitable practice throughout the six entry points. If we think about spaces, there could be overlap with systems and/or processes. When we consider relationships, it could be directly related to mindsets. These examples are provided only as a starting point for a much larger discussion within your own context, as they can help you and your team reflect on the biggest opportunities for considering where equitable practices might be considered or enhanced. The entry points for equity are a bridge to understanding what equity is and how to make it actionable in your work.

> *The entry points for equity are a bridge to understanding what equity is and how to make it actionable in your work.*

## Practice

Explore the entry points by identifying the inequity and determining possible action steps for the following situation. A teacher says, "It's hard for me to connect with a student in my class. Their name is very hard to pronounce, so I gave them a nickname — a shortened version of their first name. Ever since then, they refuse to participate in group activities."

1. To which entry point(s) does this situation align?

2. What inequities can you identify in this situation?

3. What would you suggest to the teacher?

4. What impact will your suggestions have on the situation? On the learner? On the educator?

## WHAT DO THE ENTRY POINTS LOOK LIKE IN PRACTICE?

Let's look at an example around math instruction in a school district. The school leadership team has noticed that the number of students enrolling in advanced math classes is declining year after year, which they have deemed a problem because of its impact on student enrollment, staffing in higher-level classes, and the school's overall rating. The school's position statement on math instruction is as follows:

> *We center mathematics teaching and learning on student thinking and promote an asset-based approach to guide instructional decisions. We believe that students need well-balanced instruction that focuses on all three aspects of rigor, according to the state standards.*

The district had an established stance but noticed a misalignment in student performance, which led them to infer that their beliefs were not being enacted in their classrooms. They collectively explored *what* and *why* until they reached a realization that some teachers had components of their instructional models they believed were critical to their students' learning experiences but didn't necessarily align with the district's stance.

| WHAT | WHY | WHY | WHY |
|---|---|---|---|
| *We center mathematics teaching and learning on student thinking.* | Students bring a variety of ideas and different ways of thinking to the classroom. | We value students' prior knowledge. | We want students to feel affirmed and have healthy academic identities. |
| *We promote an asset-based approach to guide instructional decisions.* | We want students to be motivated and inspired to succeed in math. | We want students to explore math with intellectual curiosity. | We want students to want to learn math. |
| *We believe that students need well-balanced instruction that focuses on all three aspects of rigor, according to the state standards.* | Students need to learn why the math is important and how to connect it to their lives. | Students should have fluency alongside conceptual and procedural knowledge. | Students can make more sense of math when their knowledge is well-rounded. |

Next, the district asked their school leaders to unpack the *whys* by assessing the degree to which they witnessed their district math stance in action. In other words, where do they see evidence of students bringing a variety of ideas and different ways of thinking to the classroom? What does that look and sound like? How do we know that students are motivated and inspired to succeed in math? What is reflected in the data? Do students see the application of math across subjects? Outside of school?

School administrators were in a position to closely examine the intersection of equity and instruction by unpacking their *whys* and looking for evidence to support or challenge the district's math stance. What they discovered was that:

- Classes were mostly lecture style, with few opportunities for students to think aloud

- "Lower" level classes had more classroom management issues

- Rooms with strong classroom management focused on routines and procedures in math

And when they asked students directly how they felt about math and which math classes they were looking forward to, there was general apathy about the learning and lack of knowledge about which classes were required or optional. The schools worked with professional-development coaches to help them name the following problems of practice and identified these inequities:

## Entry Points for Equity Guide

| AREA OF FOCUS: | Mathematics | GRADE(S): | 6–12 |
|---|---|---|---|
| **STANCE / BELIEF / POSITION STATEMENT:** | | | |
| | *We center mathematics teaching and learning on student thinking and promote an asset-based approach to guide instructional decisions. We believe that students need well-balanced instruction that focuses on all three aspects of rigor, according to the state standards.* | | |
| **PROBLEMS OF PRACTICE** | | **INEQUITIES** | **ENTRY POINT(S) FOR EQUITY** |
| District: | *How can we expand opportunities in advanced math classes to more students and reduce the amount of tracking we currently have in place for grades 6–12?* | • *Tracking doesn't give everyone opportunities to progress into higher level classes.*<br><br>• *We might not be aware of our implicit biases and beliefs that not all students can succeed in advanced math classes.* | *Systems, processes, mindsets* |
| School: | *What do we (administrators) need to help our students be more actively engaged in math class and not just passive recipients?* | • *Teachers aren't properly trained on the math curriculum.*<br><br>• *There may be low morale among students in lower-performing and/or tracked classrooms.* | *Processes, products, mindsets* |

(Continued)

*(Continued)*

| AREA OF FOCUS: | Mathematics | | GRADE(S): | 6–12 |
|---|---|---|---|---|
| **PROBLEMS OF PRACTICE** | | | **INEQUITIES** | **ENTRY POINT(S) FOR EQUITY** |
| Classroom: | | *How can teachers encourage ways of thinking, habits of thinking, and ways of doing among students?* | • *The curriculum isn't relatable to students' lived experiences or cultures.*<br><br>• *We don't have the spaces or manipulative tools to make math learning more hands-on.* | *Processes, products* |

**ACTION STEPS:**

Processes

- Reassess the professional development (PD) plan and examine when PD occurs, topics being covered, teacher surveys, and feedback data.

- Determine the extent to which math is integrated into other subjects.

Products

- Determine the extent to which the selected math tools, textbooks, and curricula provide students with opportunities that attend to conceptual understanding, procedural skill and fluency, and application to real-world contexts.

- Calculate the balance in PD between product training and pedagogical content knowledge development.

Mindsets

- Listen to how teachers explain to parents why we teach math and why it's important.

- Witness how teachers show that math is a tool for student agency.

After naming the problems of practice and identifying the inequities, and pinpointing the corresponding entry points, schools can then set goals and action steps to enact equity and address the problems of practice. As with all goals, it's important to know where you are starting. You can determine each person's level of readiness to operationalize equity by assessing their level of awareness for each inequity with the following indicators—

- This inequity is:

  - New to me. I've not seen it in action before.

  - Familiar, but I don't understand why it's an inequity.

- Making sense and I'm aware of why it's an inequity.
- One I've seen and I've helped — or witnessed others help — guide teachers toward enacting the equity.

**Teacher Commentary**

▶ This process reminds me of instructional rounds and the process of identifying the "problem of practice"! Love this . . . I can picture working with a building leadership team or district-level team and taking them through this process . . . Wow! Let's go!

▶ I love this process. It seems like it doesn't go straight to blame but instead really looks for problems of practice, inequities, and then solutions. I always assumed you start with the entry points, but in this example, we started with the problems of practice and aligned them with the entry points to help guide our solutions!

In the previous example, the district examined their belief about math instruction. Starting with the *why* is the first step in activating the entry points. *Why do we have this position, stance, or belief in place?* If your team, school, or district does not have a stated position on the topic, you can use a grounding exercise to uncover everyone's perspectives and beliefs about the topic.

Group grounding exercises are best done in a circle format so that everyone can see one another — and in small groups of less than twenty people. Participants take turns answering the questions *What do we believe?* and *Why?* After a belief is stated, the question *why* can be asked repeatedly, in succession, until no more reasons can be identified. Continue asking the *what* question until all beliefs have been stated. Everyone should have the same amount of uninterrupted speaking time to answer the questions (one or two minutes), and you should allow for people to chime in at a pace that feels comfortable for them. This type of structured call-and-response protocol brings thoughts and beliefs to the surface. You can synthesize the themes and patterns in all of the responses into a few statements that capture your belief or stance about the topic.

**Problem of practice.** The next step in activating the entry points is to connect the belief or stance to a **problem of practice**, an area that "focuses on the instructional core, is directly observable, is actionable, and connects to a broader strategy of improvement" (Learning Forward, 2022). When there is a misalignment between what you believe and what you're doing, therein lies an inequity. Your problem of practice should lead toward improved student outcomes. It can be indicated as a question or a statement. The Learning

Forward problem of practice formula is **what + who + why + where + when + how = problem of practice**. Following is an example.

**What:** expand opportunities

**Who:** for students to be in advanced math classes

**Why:** have more active engagement in math

**Where:** across grades 6–12

**When:** by the end of next school year

**How:** through helping teachers encourage ways of thinking, habits of thinking, and ways of doing

**Problem of practice:** We will expand opportunities for students to be in advanced math classes and be more actively engaged across grades 6–12 by the end of next school year through helping teachers encourage ways of thinking, habits of thinking, and ways of doing.

And here is the same problem of practice posed as questions:

- How can we expand opportunities for students to be in advanced math classes and be more actively engaged in math across grades 6–12 by the end of next school year?

- How can we prepare and support teachers in encouraging ways of thinking, habits of thinking, and ways of doing among their students?

## Teacher Pro-Tip

Pose the problem of practice as a question because approaching an issue from a place of inquiry opens you and your team up to ideating more creative solutions. Connecting the position, stance, or belief to the problem of practice is like linking a positive and negative charge to create an electric spark. The spark of conversation is what activates the entry points for equity. Entering the equity conversation from a place of inquiry, with specific questions, gives you a safe space to discover things that aren't yet understood and to hear differing perspectives. Powerful questions will allow you and your team to make more personal connections to the issue.

When you ideate solutions to the issue, you're identifying the inequities related to the problem. Avoid defensive stances by keeping students at the center of the conversation. *How is this impacting our students?* Modifying the Learning Forward problem of practice model, we can begin to identify inequities:

What *must end or can no longer be tolerated* +

Who *is being disadvantaged and/or wronged* +

Why *is this a problem* +

Where *is this happening* +

When *does this surface* +

How *was it maintained and sustained*

= **Inequities**

Here is an example:

What *must end or can no longer be tolerated* +

**students being tracked into math classes with lower expectations**

Who *is being disadvantaged and/or wronged* +

**students in lower-level classes**

Why *is this a problem* +

**future might be limited by lack of access to higher-level classes**

Where *is this happening* +

**Grades 6–12**

When *does this surface* +

**day-to-day behaviors that show we don't believe in all of our students**

How *was it maintained and sustained*

**low morale among students**

= **Inequities**

And these are the stated inequities:

- Tracking doesn't give everyone opportunities to progress into higher-level classes.

- We must have implicit biases and beliefs that not all students can succeed in advanced math classes.

- Teachers aren't properly trained on use of the math curriculum.

- There may be low morale among students in lower-performing and/or tracked classrooms.

- The curriculum isn't relatable to students' lived experiences or cultures.

- We don't have the spaces or manipulative tools to make math learning more hands-on.

**Note:** Tracking and ability grouping of students is a controversial issue that is not without systemic inequities. Exploring this topic through the entry points of equity can provide structure to very soulful dialogues.

## Teacher Commentary

This section encapsulates what I battled when teaching high school. Teachers and admins wanted more remediation and tracking. They didn't want to face the inequities head-on by providing more opportunities and more access. I got no support from admins at the building or district level. If I could go back in time, I'd work with my team to identify our problems of practice and really try to help shift the mindsets of our leadership.

## ENTRY POINT IN ACTION

Earlier in this book, I recalled my first year of teaching and how biased I was toward the girls in my classroom, which was a huge inequity. I imagine that I often made the boys feel ignored or less important. Once I realized the inequity, I was honest and up-front with my students. I told them about my tendency to call on girls more than boys and why that was wrong. I explained that as much as I love teaching middle schoolers, I am always perplexed at the differences in our human nature. And then I took action by asking my students to be accountability partners with me — letting me know when I was exhibiting biased behavior. One student volunteered to collect data for a day on how often I called on girls versus boys! I was elated to see such math in action! And guess what? I changed my behaviors. Yes, it took time to break a bad habit but not a long time because I had a clear goal and intentions. Here's how I could have approached my situation using the entry points for equity.

## Entry Points for Equity Guide

| AREA OF FOCUS: | Mathematics | GRADE(S): | | 7 |
|---|---|---|---|---|
| **STANCE / BELIEF / POSITION STATEMENT:** | | | | |
| | *Every student's perspective, ideas, and thoughts are equally valid and deserve to be heard and affirmed.* | | | |
| **PROBLEMS OF PRACTICE** | | **INEQUITIES** | **ENTRY POINT(S) FOR EQUITY** | |
| Classroom: | *How can I ensure equity of voice among students?* | • *Boys are not called on as often as girls* | *Processes, mindsets* | |
| **ACTION STEPS:** | | | | |

Processes

- Collect data for a day on how often I called on girls versus boys
- Check in with students (during class meeting or using question box) to see if they feel affirmed and recognized

Mindsets

- Collaborate with grade-level team to discuss and learn about student behaviors more often

## Practice

Review the following scenario about students' perceptions of a district's assessment processes. Complete the *Entry Points for Equity Guide* with a colleague or group of peers. This exercise will help you gauge your readiness to recognize inequities and come up with solutions.

The Exchange Quest School District has a history of showing poor test scores for Black and minority students and misusing state assessments for school and teacher accountability. Schools in the district focused their test preparation efforts on students on the cusp of proficiency, but the result was that students began showing evidence of high stress related to tests and developing negative perceptions of the word *assessment*. In an effort to make positive change, the district set an expectation to include students in the assessment processes so that they would feel more ownership over assessments and so teachers would adopt assessment *as* learning rather than only using assessment *of* learning. The ninth- and tenth-grade team of teachers at one particular school in the district, Hope High School, shifted their assessment practices by moving away from assessments being events or single tests to embedding assessment processes throughout the entire teaching and learning cycle. Teachers were intentionally transparent with students about when, how, and why assessment processes were being used, whether they were

- formative assessment practices such as methods to clarify learning, ways to elicit evidence of what students know, or things like exit tickets and feedback, or
- single-event tests such as quizzes, interim or summative tests, or unit projects.

After a year of employing assessment processes and adopting assessment *as* learning, students were asked questions about assessments to see if they were grasping the district's shift in assessment practices. Here is what the students said when asked what they think about when they hear the word *assessment*.

- Olon, Grade 9 — Usually, when I hear the word assessment, I think of a test, but I just group assessments and tests and quizzes in the same category. I think teachers need to avoid making the room super-tense during the tests.
- Flannery, Grade 10 — When I hear the word assessment, I usually think about how many points it's worth and when the assessment is going to happen. . . . I think so much about my grade, and I really want to give it my all. I wish my teachers would avoid putting how many points each question is worth on assessments. I feel like it just adds so much more pressure because I don't feel confident.

## Entry Points for Equity Guide

| AREA OF FOCUS: | | GRADE(S): | |
|---|---|---|---|
| STANCE / BELIEF / POSITION STATEMENT: | | | |
| | | | |

|  | PROBLEMS OF PRACTICE | INEQUITIES | ENTRY POINT(S) FOR EQUITY |
|---|---|---|---|
| District: | | | |
| School: | | | |
| Classroom: | | | |

## A TEACHER'S EXAMPLE: BANNING BOOKS

As an ELA department head, part of my job was selecting books to read in ELA classes and fielding concerns about the books from students and families. One spring, a group of parents and students expressed concern about a certain title.

The parents and students happened to represent a religious community that had a reputation for banning books due to what they categorized as inappropriate content. With that information in mind, I was prepared to argue vehemently against book censorship. But I made sure to listen to the parents' and students' concerns.

Parents argued that they just wanted a heads-up about the intense content that occurred in the beginning of the book so that they could help prepare for and navigate that content appropriately with their students at home. They didn't use the words *trigger warning*, but that's what they were advocating for — and they were exactly right. There were probably several other students outside of their religious community who needed that heads-up as well.

By listening to their concerns instead of leaping to assumptions, I learned to accept a suggestion that benefited the parents' and students' community as well as the student community overall. From that meeting forward, I continued to learn how to engage students and families in exchanging ideas that would help students navigate intense content coming up in the texts that we were using.

Upon reflection, here's how I applied the steps outlined in this chapter:

1. Student and family perspectives need to be considered to inform materials used in teaching and learning. I assumed reasons for family and student pushback about a particular book.
2. **Inequities:** Initially, I missed out on valuable perspectives that could benefit the whole student community.
3. **Entry points:** Mindset, processes

4. **Action steps:**
   - **Mindset:** Interrupt assumptions about why the family and student group were raising concerns about book choices.

   - **Processes:** Continuously engage in check-ins with families and students to know more about concerns. Use information to create book options that benefit student success *and* well-being.

Imagine that you have the opportunity to engage in dialogue with this teacher. You two will discuss their perception of the situation at their school and determine if the inequities and action steps are solutions that will lead toward equitable solutions for students. Write your responses to the following questions, as if you were preparing to talk with the teacher.

- Does the teacher understand what must end or can no longer be tolerated? Why, or why not?

  _____

  _____

  _____

- Has the teacher identified who is being disadvantaged and/or wronged?

  _____

  _____

  _____

- Do you think the teacher identified the correct problem? How is the problem defined?

  _____

  _____

  _____

- How might students or families explain the problem? What else might they say?

  _____

  _____

  _____

- Will the outlined action steps meet the needs of students, families, and educators? Why, or why not?

_____

_____

_____

- What is a similar experience that you can share with the teacher? Explain how that experience taught you a valuable lesson.

_____

_____

_____

## HOW CAN WE USE ENTRY POINTS TO ACT ON EQUITY?

Equity will always be a key component of teaching and learning, and the entry points for equity help us talk about equity and make it a priority in our work. The following are suggestions on what to consider as you interact with the six entry points for equity.

**Mindsets.** Educators' mental attitudes, along with how their empowering or disempowering beliefs about students can impact their teaching and learning. Beliefs about content, pedagogy, and students can influence teaching and instructional decision-making. *Consider: Where are you on the continuum of equity? What are your levels of readiness to operationalize equity?*

**Relationships.** Building and maintaining psychologically safe relationships with students is critical. Knowing that all relationships begin with the self, educators should explore how their experiences as learners shaped how they think about education, how they engage with content, and what they believe about their students' potential. *Consider: How do you ensure that relationships with students, educators, and stakeholders are psychologically safe and learner oriented? How do you ensure that these relationships promote collaborative inquiry?*

**Products.** Access to rigorous content and high-quality instructional materials is essential for equitable teaching. Educators need ample time to examine the tools used to support teaching and learning, such as curricula, text, and digital programs. *Consider: Are the products that support your teaching and learning affirming for students? Do they invite students to engage with meaning? Do they reflect ideas and experiences that your learners will recognize?*

**Spaces.** Students' identities are strengthened when they feel a sense of belonging and when their identities are affirmed and validated. Educators should intentionally design and examine the environment they create for learning from a student's perspective. *Consider: What messages does your space convey to your learners?*

**Processes.** Assess the routines, procedures, and protocols used in day-to-day teaching and learning. A greater opportunity for equitable teaching and learning exists when we view assessment as learning — a process that ensures the learner understands what they're learning, how they are learning it, and why they are learning it. *Consider: What steps can you take to embrace assessment as learning with your students? How can you help students better understand their role in the assessment process? What are practical ways to increase student agency?*

**Systems.** Each school or district has essential systems in place to serve students. These structures range from how teachers are evaluated to how students are greeted at the door. *Consider: How are you supporting your teachers so that they are best equipped to help all kids learn? What learning pathways are designed for teachers' continuous learning and development in the areas of academic and professional standards, pedagogy, and content knowledge? Does this guidance align with your current beliefs and practices?*

To do equity work respectfully and honorably, we must be willing to be honest and say things that might make others feel uncomfortable. Similarly, we must be willing to experience discomfort ourselves. Set the expectation for you and your team to get comfortable with the discomfort because (1) students — and others experiencing inequities — have been uncomfortable and (2) growth begins outside of your comfort zone.

# EPILOGUE

Dear Reader,

Attending to the work of equity means being deliberate in raising your awareness of self and others, exploring your beliefs, and examining your actions. You've just completed incredible inner work. Self-reflection is like a muscle, and you've gotten stronger by completing the reflection exercises in this book. Consider what's different about how you are thinking about equity now that you've completed *The Equity Expression.* Recognize and celebrate your growth!

If you approached the text with an intent to learn and grow, you've undoubtedly gleaned additional insights on equity-related issues. I hope that this book inspired you to make self-reflection an ongoing part of your practice, and encouraged you to connect deeply with your inner self. Reflection gives you more control over your experiences because you become more aware of the beliefs and fears that drive your decision making, and it becomes easier to figure out what to do with your beliefs, fears, doubts, questions, and certainties about equity. This self-awareness is the first step toward positive change.

Operationalizing equity requires courageous discussions and deep reflection, both within you and with others. You will encounter people that agree with you, and those with whom you disagree. People have different beliefs that help them make sense of the world and make life feel sensible. Our beliefs can sometimes make us feel safe. Problems occur when we begin to judge other people's beliefs, or when those beliefs do harm to others. I trust that you are more equipped to serve as an equity-empowered educator that accepts people where they are, and who models equitable practices for others to witness. You do this work for yourself, for other educators, and, most importantly, for our students. I hope that this book encouraged you to have more compassion toward others.

As educators, we have the responsibility to engage in equity conversations to make sure all students have an opportunity to succeed and thrive in their schooling. My hope is that the suggestions I provided in this book will complement and enrich your equity work, enhance your professional development experiences, and support you in being a deeply reflective, equity-empowered educator. My hope is that you will reveal and unlock greater potential in you and in others wherever learning takes place.

May the inner work you've done by reading this book help you to fan your flames, and keep ablaze your fire—for teaching, for learning, for an equitable and excellent education for our students. May the embers that radiate from your equity work uncover and unearth our passions for helping all students succeed!

Congratulations!

Yours, in equity,
Fenesha

*PS. If you feel that you're still not quite ready to meet with your colleagues and continue this work because you might be too emotionally charged, allow yourself time to* **consciously complain**—*either to someone else, or alone. Complaining is easy, but doing it consciously means that you not only state the complaint (or yell it, if you prefer), but you attach specific emotions and feelings to it so that you become even more aware of what's inside of you that needs to be released. Remember, feelings are invitations to welcome growth and change. You've got this.*

# GLOSSARY OF TERMS

**180-partner:** This colleague is a person you imagine to be 180 degrees different than you—perhaps in your upbringing, cultural experiences, or even subjects that you teach. If you teach math, your 180-partner might be an ELA teacher. The purpose of selecting a 180-partner is to engage in conversation where you will learn from the insight and experience of someone different from you.

**360-partner:** This colleague is a person you imagine you can relate to because they are aligned in what you teach, your cultural experiences or background, and interests. If you teach sixth-grade science, your 360-partner might be the eighth-grade science teacher. The purpose of selecting a 360-partner is to engage in conversation where it might be easier to converse on topics because you have a common ground.

**academic identity:** The dispositions and beliefs that make up a person's relationship with a topic or subject.

**assessment as learning:** A process in which assessment occurs simultaneously with learning. (Yan, 2021)

**assessment for learning:** A process in which assessment occurs before learning. (Yan, 2021)

**assessment of learning:** A process in which assessment occurs after learning. (Yan, 2021)

**assessment process:** A collection of integrated and iterative actions informed by and responsive to students. Assessment processes include creating human-centered learning conditions, identifying and sharing learning goals, and using quality tools as well as evidence (data) analysis protocols to inform learning decisions.

**bias:** A conscious or unconscious "tendency to believe that some people, ideas, etc., are better than others that usually results in treating some people unfairly." Common kinds of bias include ability, gender expression, gender identity, linguistic, race, sex, and socioeconomic status.

**consciously complain:** This intentional relationship practice is a complaining technique that helps you clear the air and be emotionally honest in the presence of others, and it sets healthy behavioral boundaries around a behavior that's usually unconscious and unrewarding. In this practice, [you take] responsibility for learning how to name and listen to your own emotions, and this will add immeasurably to your emotional skills. (McLaren, 2020)

**cultural archetype:** A similar set of beliefs, values, or behaviors that show up in different cultures. (Hammond, 2015, p. 156)

**culturally responsive teachers:** Culturally responsive teachers have unequivocal faith in the human dignity and intellectual capabilities of their students. They view learning as having intellectual, academic, personal, social, ethical, and political dimensions, all of which are developed in concert with one another. (Gay, 2000)

**culturally responsive teaching:** "The process of using familiar cultural information and processes to scaffold learning. Emphasizes communal orientation. Focused on relationships, cognitive scaffolding, and critical social awareness." (Hammond 2015, p. 156) deficit thinking: Deficit thinking refers to the idea or worldview that particular students fail in school because the students and their families have "deficits" that impede their learning (for example, limited education, poverty, minority status). (Gorski, 2010)

educator: More inclusive than "teacher," it takes the collaboration of many educational professionals to make impactful and meaningful learning experiences for students. Taking an integrated approach to teaching and learning requires collective work and responsibility.

entry point: Describes how we are most likely to experience a big topic in our daily lives.

equity: The fair treatment, access, opportunity, and advancement for all, that facilitate their individual success and belonging. Equity identifies and eliminates the barriers to access and opportunities that put students at a disadvantage.

formative assessment: A planned, ongoing process used by all students and teachers during learning and teaching to elicit and use evidence of student learning to improve student understanding of intended disciplinary learning outcomes and support students to become self-directed learners. (Council of Chief State Officers, 2013)

formative assessment purpose: Formative assessment processes are a blend of both planned and in-the-moment actions and responses. When educators and students partner to effectively use these practices, they gain proven and powerful levers to achieve equitable teaching and learning outcomes, including academic achievement, well-being, and self-efficacy.

funds of knowledge: "Collections of knowledge based in . . . practices that are a part of families' inner culture, work experience, or daily routine. It is the knowledge and expertise that students and their family members have because of their roles and experiences in their families, communities, and culture." (No Time For Flash Cards, 2018)

InTASC Standards: Model Core Teaching Standards that outline what teachers should know and be able to do to ensure every PK–12 student reaches the goal of being ready to enter college or the workforce in today's world. This "common core" outlines the principles and foundations of teaching practice that cut across all subject areas and grade levels and that all teachers share. (Council of Chief State Officers, 2023)

intellectual capacity: The increased power the brain creates to process complex information more effectively. (Hammond, 2015, p. 16)

interim assessment purpose: To provide information about where students are in their learning and how they're growing toward benchmarks. Results from interim assessments can be used to help educators (including leaders) and learners make responsive decisions. Interim assessment processes occur at intervals (e.g., every six to eight weeks).

learner: Alternative term for "student." To support our young people in attaining their full potential as thriving individuals with healthy academic identities and agency we acknowledge that students are more than just recipients of knowledge, but rather co-owners of their learning.

learner context: Background information about learners that informs responsive-teaching-and-learning actions and decisions. Educators and learners collaboratively gather this information (data) and use it to keep the student at the center of teaching and learning processes. Learner context consists of family, community, historical, and other contexts, funds of knowledge, identities, interests, needs, and strengths.

learner empowerer: A mindset and resulting practices based on twenty-first-century expectations for teaching, learning, and assessment. Processes are applied with learners, promoting their success, well-being, and self-efficacy.

learning environment: A place where individual and collaborative learning occurs, including traditional spaces, such as classrooms, and other educational settings. Nurturing learning environments and relationships are important actions derived from these two responsive learning cycle practices: embracing learner context and strengthening learning culture.

microaggression: Subtle, everyday verbal and nonverbal slights, snubs, or insults which communicate hostile, derogatory, or negative messages to people of color based solely on their marginalized group membership. (Hammond, 2015, p. 47).

mindset: A set of mental attitudes that determines how one will interpret and respond to situations (Hammond, 2015, p. 157); the set of assumptions, values, and beliefs about oneself and the world that influences how one perceives, interprets, and acts upon one's environment. (Dweck, 1999)

pedagogical beliefs: Things that an educator accepts as true about their teaching and learning practices and process to help students learn.

pedagogical content knowledge: The ability to translate subject matter to a diverse group of students using multiple strategies and methods of instruction and assessment while understanding the contextual [and] cultural . . . [conditions] within the learning environment. (Veal & MaKinster, 1999)

problem of practice: An area that a school or school district identifies that focuses on the instructional core, is directly observable, is actionable, and connects to a broader strategy of improvement. (Learning Forward, n.d.)

school-to-prison pipeline: A set of seemingly unconnected school policies and teacher instructional decisions that over time results in students of color not receiving adequate literacy and content instruction while being disproportionately disciplined for non-specific, subjective offenses such as "defiance." (Hammond, 2015, p. 13)

structural equity: Redesigning systems and structures without investing in the deeper personal, interpersonal, and cultural shifts. (Safir & Dugan, 2021, p. 33)

student agency: Structures, process, practices, and behaviors that give students voice in how they learn, which empowers them to influence their own path to mastery. (Reese, n.d.)

summative assessment purpose: To provide processes used to certify learning, often at the end of a set of lessons, unit, or course. In contrast with formative assessment, summative processes are evaluative in nature and may help make determinations in grading, reporting, placement, and improvement in teaching and learning.

teaching and learning: A holistic perspective to the process we engage in with students that accounts for the intellectual, academic, personal, cultural, and social dimensions that learners bring to the learning environment.

weaponization of data: The use of assessment processes, tools, or results in ways that disempower learners or educators and contributes to or perpetuates educational disparity, toxic stress, and trauma.

# FURTHER READING

## CHAPTER 1. ACADEMIC IDENTITIES

For more information on academic identities as it relates to equity-based practices, check out *The Impact of Identity in K-8 Mathematics* by Julia Aguirre, Karen Mayfield-Ingram, and Danny Bernard Martin (2013).

## CHAPTER 2. MINDSETS

For a deep-dive into how to broaden our body of explanations and interpretations of student actions, I recommend Zaretta Hammond's tools on preparing to be a culturally responsive practitioner in *Culturally Responsive Teaching and the Brain* (2015).

## CHAPTER 3. RELATIONSHIPS WITH EDUCATORS

In this chapter, I reference whiteness. Here are resources that can support your learning about how racism shapes our lives and unlearning mindsets and beliefs that have contributed to systems of oppression:

- https://www.whitesupremacyculture.info
- Showing Up For Racial Justice, surj.org
- *Caste* by Isabel Wilkerson
- *So You Want to Talk About Race* by Ijeoma Oluo

- *White Rage* by Carol Anderson

## CHAPTER 4. RELATIONSHIPS WITH STUDENTS

For additional support on how to develop relationships with students, I recommend Chapters 5 and 6 of Zaretta Hammond's *Culturally Responsive Teaching and the Brain*. Chapter 5 focuses on "Building the Foundation of Learning Partnerships" for effective student–teacher relationships and Chapter 6, "Establishing Alliance in the Learning Partnership," "explores the special stance and skills teachers need in order to leverage relationships and culture" with students (Hammond, 2015, p. 8).

## CHAPTER 5. PRODUCTS

To learn more about connecting students' home and school experiences through your use of products, I recommend that you explore the writings and teachings from pioneers of this work, Geneva Gay and Gloria Ladson-Billings. Their work addresses the role of cultural competence, critical consciousness, and diversity in teaching and learning.

## CHAPTER 6. PROCESSES

To learn more about assessment *as* learning, check out *Assessment as Learning* by Zi Yan and Lan Yang (2021).

## CHAPTER 7. SPACES

For more information on seeing the learning "environment as the second teacher," I recommend Zaretta Hammond's chapter on "Creating a Culturally Responsive Community for Learning," in *Culturally Responsive Teaching and the Brain*.

# REFERENCES

## CHAPTER 1. ACADEMIC IDENTITIES

Aguirre, J., & Del Rosario Zavala, M. (2013). Making culturally responsive mathematics teaching explicit: A lesson analysis tool. *Pedagogies: An International Journal, 8*(2), 163–190.

Aguirre, J., Mayfield-Ingram, K., & Martin, D. (2013). *The impact of identity in K–8 mathematics learning and teaching: Rethinking equity-based practices.* The National Council of Teachers of Mathematics.

Every Student Succeeds Act, 20 U.S.C. § 6301. (2015). congress.gov/114/plaws/publ95/PLAW-114publ95.pdf

Gay, G. (2000). *Culturally responsive teaching: Theory, research, and practice.* Teachers College Press.

No Child Left Behind Act of 2001, P.L. 107-110, 20 U.S.C. § 6319. (2002).

Robinson, K., & Robinson, K. (2022, March). *What is education for?* https://www.edutopia.org/article/what-education

Veal, W. R., & MaKinster, J. G. (1999). Pedagogical content knowledge taxonomies. *The Electronic Journal of Science Education, 3*(4). http://ejse.southwestern.edu/article/view/7615

## CHAPTER 2. MINDSETS

Eschmann, R., Groshek, J., Chanderdatt, R., Chang, K., & Whyte, M. (2020). Making a microaggression: Using big data and qualitative analysis to map the reproduction and disruption of microaggressions through social media. *Social Media + Society, 6*(4). https://doi.org/10.1177/2056305120975716

Fernando, C. (2021, May 4). Some Black parents say remote learning during pandemic has kept students safe from racism in classroom. *Chicago Tribune.* https://www.chicagotribune.com/coronavirus/ct-aud-nw-black-students-racism-remote-learning-20210504-yhycne3n7fdgpjdxtnavmn7yqq-story.html

Gay, G. (2018). *Culturally responsive teaching: Theory, research, and practice* (3rd ed.). Teachers College Press.

Gay, G. (2000). *Culturally responsive teaching: Theory, research, and practice.* Teachers College Press.

Gershenson, S., Holt, S. G., & Papageorge, N. W. (2016, June 1). Who believes in me? The effect of student–teacher demographic match on teacher expectations. *Economics of Education Review, 52.* http://www.fixschooldiscipline.org/wp-content/uploads/2020/09/12.Who_Believes_In_Me.2016.pdf

Hammond, Z. L. (2015). *Culturally responsive teaching and the brain.* Corwin.

Issa, N. (2022, March 31). CPS removes teacher who hung Black doll from cord in classroom. *Chicago Sun-Times.* https://chicago.suntimes.com/education/2022/3/30/23003786/whitney-young-cps-public-schools-doll-black-african-american-hung-history

Keels, M., Durkee, M. I., & Hope, E. C. (2017). The psychological and academic costs of school-based racial and ethnic micro aggressions. *American Educational Research Journal, 54*(6), 1316–1344.

Murphy, N. (2022, October 19). Before the national outrage: Why young kids need to be taught about racism. *Teach. Learn. Grow.* https://www.nwea.org/blog/2021/

before-the-national-outrage-why-young-kids-need-to-be-taught-about-racism/

NYU Steinhardt. (2022, January 26). An asset-based approach to education: What it is and why it matters. *NYU Steinhardt Teacher Residency Program.* https://teachereducation.steinhardt.nyu.edu/an-asset-based-approach-to-education-what-it-is-and-why-it-matters/

## CHAPTER 3. RELATIONSHIPS WITH EDUCATORS

Ab Rashid, R. (2018). Dialogic reflection for professional development through conversations on a social networking site. *International and Multidisciplinary Perspectives, 19*(1), 105–117.

Chasara, K. C. (2016, August 26). *Building learning organization.* https://www.academia.edu/28035668/Building_learning_organization_20_20339

Council of Chief State School Officers. (2011, April). *Interstate teacher assessment and support consortium (InTASC) model core teaching standards: A resource for state dialogue.* https://ccsso.org/sites/default/files/2017-11/InTASC_Model_Core_Teaching_Standards_2011.pdf

Darling-Hammond, L., Hyler, M. E., & Gardner, M. (2017, June). *Effective teacher professional development.* Learning Policy Institute. https://learningpolicyinstitute.org/sites/default/files/product-files/Effective_Teacher_Professional_Development_FACTSHEET.pdf

Darling-Hammond, L., Oakes, J., Wojcikiewicz, S., Hyler, M. E., Guha, R., Podolsky, A., Kini, T., Cook-Harvey, C., Mercer, C., & Harrell, A. (2019). Learning Policy Institute. *Preparing for teachers deeper learning* (Research brief). https://learningpolicyinstitute.org/product/preparing-teachers-deeper-learning-brief

Dierdorff, E. C., & Rubin, R. S. (2017, December 6). Research: We're not very self-aware, especially at work. *Harvard Business Review.* https://hbr.org/2015/03/research-were-not-very-self-aware-especially-at-work

Gay, G. (2000). *Culturally responsive teaching: Theory, research, and practice.* Teachers College Press.

Gube, M. (2022, August 25). Resilient organizations make psychological safety a strategic priority. *Harvard Business Review.* https://hbr.org/2022/08/resilient-organizations-make-psychological-safety-a-strategic-priority

Henning, K. (2021). *The rage of innocence: How America criminalizes black youth.* Vintage.

Learning Forward. (2023). *Professional expertise.* https://standards.learningforward.org/standards-for-professional-learning/rigorous-content-for-each-learner/professional-expertise/

Serrat, O. (2013). *Reflective practice.* https://www.academia.edu/11518185/Reflective_Practice

## CHAPTER 4. RELATIONSHIPS WITH STUDENTS

Gay, G. (2000). *Culturally responsive teaching: Theory, research, and practice.* Teachers College Press.

Hammond, Z. L. (2015). *Culturally responsive teaching and the brain.* Corwin.

## CHAPTER 5. PRODUCTS

Gay, G. (2000). *Culturally responsive teaching: Theory, research, and practice.* Teachers College Press.

Guarino, J., Cole, S., & Sperling, M. (2022). Our children are not numbers. *Mathematics Teacher: Learning and Teaching PK–12, 115*(6), 404–412.

## CHAPTER 6. PROCESSES

Beard, E. (2023, January 18). Student-centered assessment literacy: A conversation between two teachers. *Teach. Learn. Grow.* https://www.nwea.org/blog/2023/student-centered-assessment-literacy-a-conversation-between-two-teachers/

NWEA. (2022). *Responsive learning cycles glossary.* https://dpdol.nwea.org/pl/rlc/RLC_Glossary_FY22.pdf

# CHAPTER 7. SPACES

National Research Council. (2018). *How people learn II*. National Academies Press EBooks.

Ralph, M. (2021, March 29). How universal design for learning can help with lesson planning this year. *Edutopia*. https://blog.defined learning.com/blog/what-is-student-agency

Scott-Webber, L. (2014, November 20). *How poorly designed classroom space puts student learning at risk*. The Hechinger Report. https://hechingerreport.org/poorly-designed-classroom-space-puts-student-learning-risk/

Taylor, A., Aldrich, R. A., & Vlastos, G. (2011, September 15). *Architecture can teach ... and the lessons are rather fundamental*. https://www.context.org/iclib/ic18/taylor/

# CHAPTER 8. SYSTEMS (AND HOW TO THRIVE IN THEM)

Minnich, C. (2020, June 22). NWEA on the future of state assessment. *Teach. Learn. Grow.* https://www.nwea.org/blog/2019/nwea-on-the-future-of-state-assessment/

Safir, S., & Dugan, J. (2021). *Street data: A next-generation model for equity, pedagogy, and school transformation*. Corwin.

Tschannen-Moran, B., & Tschannen-Moran, M. (2010). *Evocative coaching: Transforming schools one conversation at a time*. Jossey-Bass.

# CHAPTER 9. ACTIVATING THE ENTRY POINTS

Learning Forward. (2022, July 20). *Standards for professional learning*. https://standards.learningforward.org/

Lipton, L., & Wellman, B. M. (2010). *Groups at work: Strategies and structures for professional learning*. Miravia.

Tschannen-Moran, B., & Tschannen-Moran, M. (2010). *Evocative coaching: Transforming schools one conversation at a time*. Jossey-Bass.

# GLOSSARY OF TERMS

Allison, C. (2022, April 19). Addressing unfinished learning in the context of grade-level work. *Peers and Pedagogy*. https://achievethecore.org/aligned/addressing-unfinished-learning-context-grade-level-work

Council of Chief State School Officers. (2013, April). InTASC learning progressions for teachers. https://ccsso.org/sites/default/files/2017-12/2013_INTASC_Learning_Progressions_for_Teachers.pdf

Council of Chief State School Officers. (2023, February 26). *Revising the definition of formative assessment*. https://ccsso.org/resource-library/revising-definition-formative-assessment

Dweck, C. S. (1999). *Mindset: The new psychology of success*. Random House.

Gorski, P. (2010). *Unlearning deficit ideology and the scornful gaze: Thoughts on authenticating the class discourse in education*. http://www.edchange.org/publications/deficit-ideology-scornful-gaze.pdf

Learning Forward. (n.d.). The Professional Learning Association. https://learningforward.org

McLaren, K. (2020, October 4). *A surprising new empathic skill: Complaining! (Consciously!)*. https://karlamclaren.com/a-surprising-new-empathic-skill-complaining-consciously/

Murphy, N. (2022, October 19). Before the national outrage: Why young kids need to be taught about racism. *Teach. Learn. Grow.* https://www.nwea.org/blog/2021/before-the-national-outrage-why-young-kids-need-to-be-taught-about-racism/

No Time For Flash Cards. (2018, February 11). *How to use funds of knowledge in your classroom and create better connections*. https://www.notimeforflashcards.com/2018/02/fundsof-knowledge.html

Reese, D. (n.d.). *What is student agency?* https://blog.definedlearning.com/blog/what-is-student-agency

Safir, S., & Dugan, J. (2021). *Street data: A next-generation model for equity, pedagogy, and school transformation*. Corwin.

Veal, W. R., & MaKinster, J. G. (1999). Pedagogical content knowledge taxonomies. *The Electronic Journal of Science Education, 3*(4), 1–9. http://ejse.southwestern.edu/article/view/7615

Yan, Z., & Yang, L. (2021). *Assessment as learning: Maximising opportunities for student learning and achievement.* Routledge.

# INDEX

# ABOUT THE AUTHOR

 **Fenesha Hubbard** has been leading K–12 professional development for the past twenty-one years. Her field experience includes being a middle school math teacher, instructional coach, workshop facilitator, and designer of professional development for NWEA and the Chicago Public Schools. Fenesha has worked in schools across the nation with a focus on math instruction and assessment practices. Her voice and work have been amplified at national conferences and on educational podcasts.

Fenesha's career motto has always been "supporting students by servicing teachers." She is passionate about creating authentic learning experiences and helping others grow. Her work connects research-driven ideas with best teaching practices, while keeping the learner at the center and humanity as the anchor.

Fenesha received a bachelor's in mathematics from the University of Illinois at Urbana-Champaign and a master's in instructional leadership from the University of Illinois at Chicago. She is a member of Sigma Gamma Rho Sorority, Inc., a leading international service organization founded by educators.

Fenesha resides in Chicago, Illinois, and will always have an Akita companion by her side.

# Continue Learning

## Personal Growth and Professional Development With Fenesha Hubbard

Ready to reach your full potential? If so, my strengths-based coaching can help you grow as the best educator you can be.

Embark on a journey of growth and transformation where you can challenge yourself and think critically about your instructional leadership practices. Whether you're an individual, team, or organization seeking change, my strengths-based coaching will help you reshape assumptions, beliefs, and mindsets, make decisions, and generate new ideas and outcomes.

Let's embrace new possibilities and grow together!

fenesha.com

# CORWIN
## A Sage Company

**CORWIN HAS ONE MISSION:** to enhance education through intentional professional learning.

We build long-term relationships with our authors, educators, clients, and associations who partner with us to develop and continuously improve the best evidence-based practices that establish and support lifelong learning.

## An enduring mission

Our mission is simple but vast: Partnering to help all kids learn®. We help kids get what they need in the classroom, so they can pursue their passions, shape their future, and realize their potential.